SOPHOCLES

Electra

SOPHOCLES

Electra

Translation with Notes, Introduction,
Interpretive Essay and Afterlife

Hanna M. Roisman
COLBY COLLEGE

Focus Classical Library
Focus Publishing
R. Pullins Company
Newburyport MA

THE FOCUS CLASSICAL LIBRARY
Series Editors • James Clauss and Stephen Esposito

Aristophanes: Acharnians • Jeffrey Henderson • 1992 • 1-58510-087-0
Aristophanes: The Birds • Jeffrey Henderson • 1999 • 0-941051-87-0
Aristophanes: Clouds • Jeffrey Henderson • 1992 • 0-941051-24-2
Aristophanes: Frogs • Henderson • 2008 • 978-1-58510-308-9
Aristophanes: Lysistrata • Jeffrey Henderson • 1988 • 0-941051-02-1
Aristophanes: Three Comedies: Acharnians, Lysistrata, Clouds • Jeffrey Henderson • 1997 • 0-941051-58-7
Euripides: The Bacchae • Stephen Esposito • 1998 • 0-941051-42-0
Euripides: Four Plays: Medea, Hippolytus, Heracles, Bacchae • Stephen Esposito, ed. • 2003 • 1-58510-048-X
Euripides: Hecuba • Robin Mitchell-Boyask • 2006 • 1-58510-148-6
Euripides: Heracles • Michael R. Halleran • 1988 • 0-941051-01-3
Euripides: Hippolytus • Michael R. Halleran • 2001 • 0-941051-86-2
Euripides: Medea • Anthony Podlecki • 2005, Revised • 0-941051-10-2
Euripides: The Trojan Women • Diskin Clay • 2005 • 1-58510-111-7
Golden Verses: Poetry of the Augustan Age • Paul T. Alessi • 2003 • 1-58510-064-1
Golden Prose in the Age of Augustus • Paul T. Alessi • 2004 • 1-58510-125-7
Hesiod: Theogony • Richard Caldwell • 1987 • 0-941051-00-5
Hesiod: Theogony & Works and Days • Stephanie Nelson • 2009 • 978-1-58510-288-4
The Homeric Hymns • Susan Shelmerdine • 1995 • 1-58510-019-6
Ovid: Metamorphoses • Z. Philip Ambrose • 2004 • 1-58510-103-6
Plautus: Captivi, Amphitryon, Casina, Pseudolus • David Christenson • 2008 • 978-1-58510-155-9
Sophocles: Antigone • Ruby Blondell • 1998 • 0-941051-25-0
Sophocles: Electra • Hanna M. Roisman • 2008 • 978-1-58510-281-5
Sophocles: King Oidipous • Ruby Blondell • 2002 • 1-58510-060-9
Sophocles: Oidipous at Colonus • Ruby Blondell • 2003 Revised • 1-58510-065-X
Sophocles: Philoktetes • Seth Schein • 2003 • 1-58510-086-2
Sophocles: The Theban Plays • Ruby Blondell • 2002 • 1-58510-037-4
Terence: Brothers (Adelphoe) • Charles Mercier • 1998 • 0-941051-72-2 [VHS • 0-941051-73-0]
Vergil: The Aeneid • Richard Caldwell • 2004 • 1-58510-077-3

Table of Contents

For My Beloved Yossi, Elad, and Shalev Roisman

And in Blessed Memory of My Nephew
Dani Elan Rom

PREFACE

Sophocles' *Electra* was the first play I read in Greek, but the years that passed have not made it any less of a challenge for me. Each reading of this tragedy presents new questions, provokes doubts about previous interpretations, and demands new scrutiny. I enjoyed writing this book, yet I still do not have absolute answers to the troubling feeling with which a reader is left after reading this drama about matricide. If the book brings the reader to delve further into the many questions the play raises about matricidal revenge and the motives that prompt it, it has achieved its goal.

The book is intended mainly for students and non-professionals. The Introduction discusses briefly the Greek theater and performance, the myth of Electra, and Aeschylus' and Euripides' treatments of the myth. It also briefly notes the scholarly debate regarding the play's judgment of the matricidal revenge it dramatizes and presents some of the issues of concern in the translation of the play. The translation, which aims to combine readability with fidelity to the Greek, is accompanied by notes aimed at helping the reader with the play's mythic, historical, cultural and literary aspects. In the Interpretative Essay, I present my own reading of the play, and in the Afterlife a brief account of the legacy of Sophocles' treatment of the myth. I was unfortunately unable to consult the most recent and substantial commentary, by P.J. Finglass, *Electra: Sophocles edited with introduction and commentary* (Cambridge, UK , New York: Cambridge University Press, 2007), since it arrived at my college library only after the completion of my manuscript.

I owe thanks first to the many students who studied Greek drama with me over the years. Their original thinking and questioning of accepted views made me repeatedly reconsider my interpretations and look at the play for fresh perspectives. I owe special thanks to my friend and editor Dr. Toby Mostysser for her many insights and probing questions, and for her invaluable help in turning my manuscript into a readable text. My friend Cecilia Luschnig read the entire manuscript (excluding the notes), and I owe much to her level-headed and helpful comments. I would like to thank Karen Gillum who copy-edited the manuscript with great care and saved me from many embarrassing mistakes.

1

Last but not least, I am deeply indebted to my husband Yossi Roisman, my sons Elad Roisman and Shalev Roisman, and my good friend Beatrice Rosenberg, on whom I can always rely for encouragement and support.

INTRODUCTION

Theater and Performance

Electra is one of Sophocles' seven extant plays, out of an opus of over 120. Sophocles (496-406 BCE) himself is one of only three classical Greek dramatists, along with Aeschylus (525-456 BCE) and Euripides (480-406 BCE), whose plays have survived.[1] The fate of the theater or theaters where the plays were performed is similar.

Records indicate that *Electra*, like most of the extant Greek tragedies, was performed at the City Dionysia (or Great Dionysia) of Athens, a religious festival held in late March in honor of Dionysus, god of wine and vegetation. This was the largest and most magnificent of Athens' annual state-sponsored religious festivals. By the time the *Electra* was performed, it had become a major Greek festival with an international audience.[2]

On each of three days of the festival, a different playwright mounted three tragedies, followed by a satyr play. The three tragedies, or trilogy, could tell a single story or different ones, as most probably did. The satyr play was a raucous production, rife with obscenity, which provided relief from the emotional intensity of the tragedies.[3]

Like the rest of the festival, the tragedies were sponsored by the state and their production overseen by the *archon eponymos*. This official selected the year's tragedians from among the contestants and assigned each the *choregos* (literally chorus leader, in effect financer and producer)[4] who would mount his plays and, later in the century, the actors who would perform in them. From the mid-fifth century on, the state paid the lead actors and the tragedians. While the playwrights were not quite state employees, they were not independent of the state either.

Being state sponsored, the plays had a strong didactic element. They familiarized the public with the myths that comprised their cultural heritage and engaged them in considering the myths' meanings and implications.

---

1 On Greek tragedy, see Sommerstein (2002). On Greek theater, see Ley (2006).

2 On the Dionysia, see Csapo and Slater (1995)103-121, 287.

3 On the satyr plays, see Sutton (1980)

4 On the institution of the *choregoi*, see Wilson (2000).

The involvement of the state seems to have ensured that the issues treated in the plays were of public interest, and probably defined the outer boundaries to the questioning and criticism found in many of the plays.[5] It did not, however, have the stultifying effect one might expect. The plays were produced before huge audiences of between 15,000 and 20,000 spectators. The first few rows of the theater were occupied by the elite,[6] but most of the audience consisted of the ordinary citizens of Athens—by definition adult males—though women and boys were also permitted to attend the tragic performances.[7] From the middle of the fifth century, tickets were subsidized for those who could not afford them.

The plays were part of the formal competitions that were held at the festival. They were judged by a panel formed through a combination of selection and lot.[8] Although the judges were probably chosen from among the educated elite, they were often swayed, even intimidated, by the reactions of the audiences[9] — making it likely that the winning playwrights were appreciated by the ordinary folk as well as by the upper tiers. (Sophocles won some twenty first prizes in his sixty-two years as a playwright.)

Thus classical Greek drama was also popular drama, in the best sense of the term: drama written not for the elite, but for the entire *polis*, which moved the ordinary Athenians of the time, addressed their concerns, and was fairly congruous with their thinking and world-view.

The plays were performed in the open air Theater of Dionysus, on the southeast slopes of the Acropolis. The performances began in the early morning and continued, with breaks, through the day. The performing area, located on a leveled space at the bottom of the hillside, consisted of a large *orchestra*,[10] or dancing place, for the Chorus and a narrow, elevated platform that served as a stage for the actors and was connected to the orchestra by several steps in the center.

Behind the playing area stood a stage-building, about twelve meters long and four meters high. It was termed a *skênê*, after its origin as a tent or hut. When *Electra* was produced, it was probably still a temporary wooden structure that could be dismantled after the festival. Most of the action

---

5 See Griffin (1999) on the impact of the historical events and democratic ideology of fifth century Athens on the tragic drama.

6 See also Csapo and Slater (1995) 289-290.

7 On women in the audience, see Csapo and Slater (1995) 286-287, 290-293; Taplin (1978)193-194.

8 Pickard-Cambridge (1988) 96-98. For the problematics of the lottery and the decision procedure, see Csapo and Slater (1995) 158-160.

9 Pickard-Cambridge (1988) 97-98.

10 Wiles (1997) 44-52 maintains the *orchestra* was circular; others, that it was rectangular or trapezoidal.

took place in the outdoor space in front of the *skênê*, with off-stage actions occurring inside the structure, which also served as a changing room and storage space. The *skênê* represented whatever edifice the play referred to (e.g., palace, temple, cottage, cave, etc.). It had a doorway in the middle and possibly two smaller doors, one at each side, for the actors to pass between the outdoor and indoor spaces. On either side of the *orchestra*, running up to the stage-building, were two broad aisles, referred to as *eisodoi* or *parodoi,* which served as entrances for the Chorus and characters arriving from the outside.

The seating area was large enough to seat all the 15,000 to 20,000 spectators. Stage furniture was minimal. According to Aristotle (*Poetics* 1449a16), Sophocles introduced scene painting (*skênographia*) done on cloth or wooden panels. Since most of the audience sat too far away to see the details, we can assume that the painting depicted little more than the type of location (e.g., urban, rural, seashore) and the type of edifice the stage-building represented.

Greek tragedies can be described as verse musicals. The entire script was in verse of various types. Most was in iambic trimeter, conventionally the meter of speech, which served as the basis for the spoken dialogues and monologues. The rest consisted of recitative (declamatory chanting) and of song in a variety of lyric meters, accompanied by double reed flutes and dancing. Every Greek tragedy featured a chorus, initially of twelve members, later fifteen, who danced and sang, whether alone or in dialogues (termed *kommoi*) with the other characters.

The structure of Greek tragedy is fairly predictable. It typically begins with a *prologos* (prologue, 1-120), which sets the scene and provides the background to the action. The *prologos* ends with the entrance of the chorus, singing their entry song, or *parodos* (accompanying song), which provides additional background information and strikes the play's key emotional chord – pathos for the suffering heroine in *Electra* (121-250). The rest of the play consists of *epeisodia* (episodes or scenes) separated by antiphonal odes *(stasimons* or *stasima*) sung by the chorus. Sophocles' *Electra* has four *epeisodion—stasimon* pairs (251-515, 516-870, 871-1097, 1098-1397). The action is brought to a height and the tensions resolved in the last episode, termed the *exodus,* which usually ends with a brief choral song (1398-1510). The tragedians also observe conventions of plot and character. Most of the plots were based on well-known myths. The main characters were larger-than-life mythical figures: usually great warriors or members of ruling houses. The plays were thus invested with a primal quality that is inherent in myth.

The Chorus consisted of characters from all walks of life; in *Electra*, they were well-born Argive women. Speaking with one voice, the Chorus provided information, commented on the action, and sometimes participated in the action as well. It generally expressed the normative view—which may or may not have been the playwright's. The action, as Aristotle would observe a century later, was usually compacted into a single day and restricted to a single place. These conventions meant that the dramatized action was generally the culmination of events before the play started, which the playwright had to relate to the audience without boring them. Violence was rarely displayed on stage, but usually recounted by the Chorus or a messenger. In *Electra*, the revenge murder is overheard from inside the palace.

Classical Greek tragedy was formal, stylized, non-realistic, and removed from the everyday. Both the actors and Chorus wore masks which completely covered their heads in front and back, with openings only for the eyes and mouth. The tragic costume consisted of a tunic and two mantles, one long and one short, and was worn by nearly all the characters. The masks and costumes identified the plays as tragedies, as opposed to comedies, and as dramas, as opposed to 'real life.' Along with the minimalist scenery and props, the formal structure, and the mythological background, they announced that the events portrayed took place in another realm, beyond the mundane.

Early Greek tragedies were performed with two speaking actors and one or two non-speaking mutes. Aristotle credits Sophocles with adding a third speaking actor (*Poetics* 1449a17). The lead actor was termed the *protagonist*, the second the *deuteragonist*, and the third, the *tritagonist*. All the actors were male. Since the tragedies routinely had more characters than actors, actors played multiple roles. The masks were obviously an asset here.

The most important quality required of an actor was a strong and versatile voice.[11] The huge size and open air venue of the Theater of Dionysus meant that the actors had to project very well in order to be heard. Versatility of voice was essential to endow each of the multiple characters the actor played— of whatever age or gender — with his or her distinct vocal signature and to express variations in emotion through the fixed character masks. The protagonist also had to have a good solo voice that was strong enough to stand out clearly from the singing of the choral group, with whom he sang antiphonally. Thus, the protagonist played the part that required the greatest flexibility of voice, which was not always the one that had the most lines. Sophocles' Electra was probably played by the protagonist.

The tragedies have come down to us without stage directions.[12] Since the poets directed — and often acted in — their own plays (tradition has it

---

11 Cf. Hall (2002) "The Singing Actors" on the function of the voice. Also Pavlovskis (1977) 113; Owen (1936) 148-154; Damen (1989) 318, who offers a para-dramatic treatment of the actors and the roles they play.

12 For further discussion, see Taplin (1978) 16-19, 179. For the play's staging in ancient times, see J.M. Walton, "Sophocles' Electra: Actors in Space," in Dunn (1996) 44-48.

that Sophocles had to stop performing because of a weak voice) and were on the spot to give instructions, written stage directions would have served no purpose. Thus, for us, the plays' staging is a matter of surmise, deduced from information provide by the characters so that the audience will know who and where they are and what they are doing.

In *Electra*, Sophocles has Orestes' aged tutor, the Paedagogus, open the play by identifying Orestes by his patrimony and informing him and the audience that they are standing in front of Orestes' childhood home, the royal palace represented by the *skênê*, in Argos, flanked by Hera's temple and the marketplace. We may surmise from his statements that Orestes is a young man, no longer a child, but not yet fully mature either. Electra, who emerges from the central doors of the *skênê* in line 86, provides her own verbal clues. She identifies herself by saying that she is still lamenting her father's murder and planning revenge. From the development of the plot, we can glean that she is on-stage for almost the entire performance, with only a fourteen-line exit into the palace (1384-97) toward the end of the play. Her position in front of the palace gate is remarked on by Chrysothemis (328-29) and Clytemnestra (516).

The ancient Greek audience were probably more attentive than their modern counterparts to the words and ideas of the drama. They would have had to listen carefully to follow the verbal scene painting, extensive background information, and, in Sophocles' plays, philosophical discussions. The sparse scenery, absence of on-stage violence, and difficulty of seeing the actors' movements clearly from a distance would have increased the salience of the words, while the dance and music would have augmented their emotional power.

The Myth

Sophocles' *Electra* is based on the myths telling of the succession of afflictions that befell the House of Atreus. These began with what Sophocles' Chorus refer to as "Pelops' ancient horsemanship" and the drowning of the charioteer Mytrilus (504-515). This incident involved Pelops' double treachery. The first was against the king Oenomaus, whom he had to beat in a chariot race in order to obtain the hand of his daughter, Hippodamia. To this end, he bribed Mytrilus, Oenomaus' charioteer, to remove the linchpin from a wheel of his master's chariot. This was done, and Oenomaus was killed when the wheel fell off his chariot as he raced. The second treachery was against Mytrilus. Instead of giving him the bribe he had promised (Hippodamia to lie with), Pelops threw him into the sea. Before he died, Mytrilus cursed Pelops and his descendants.

The workings of the curse begin in the next generation with Pelops' sons, Atreus and Thyestes, the fathers respectively of Agamemnon and Aegisthus. At the beginning of the play, the Paedagogus identifies the place where he and Orestes are standing as "the palace of Pelops' sons, plagued by disasters" (10). The disasters refer to the various killings and other atrocities that took place before the play's start and that ultimately lead to the double revenge at its end. The first atrocity was Atreus' butchery of Thyestes' sons and his serving their flesh to Thyestes in a cannibalistic feast in revenge for Thyestes' seduction of his wife. When Thyestes realized what he had eaten, he called down his own curse on Atreus' house. This curse was actualized in a succession of disasters: Agamemnon, on his way to fight in the Trojan War, was forced to sacrifice his daughter Iphigenia to recompense the goddess Artemis for a wrong he had inadvertently done her. On returning home, Agamemnon himself was murdered by his wife Clytemnestra and her lover, Aegisthus. Sophocles' *Electra* focuses on the last installment in this curse: the revenge taken by Agamemnon's children on their mother and her lover.

Like the other ancient playwrights, Sophocles provided his audience with the mythical information they needed to follow the dramatized events. Like them, he highlighted some details, blurred others, and relied on the audience to fill in with their own knowledge. To note only a few of many examples: he does not explicitly mention Pelops' treacheries, Agamemnon and Aegisthus being first cousins, Atreus' butchery and cannibalistic feast, the acts of Thyestes that led up to it, or the reasons that Aegisthus might have for hating Agamemnon. The questions of what details of the myth the audience would and would not have known and which of these are actually relevant to the play have long been a matter of scholarly debate.

In fact, since most of the mythic lore available to the tragedians, like most of the tragedies themselves, has been lost, we have only the most partial knowledge of the mythic material available to Sophocles when he wrote his *Electra*. The only complete works we have that refer to the revenge for Agamemnon's murder and the events leading up to it are the Homeric epics and Pindar's (b. ca 518) ode to Thrasydaeus (*Pythian* 11) composed several centuries later, and both of these treat the matter rather briefly. Of the other literary treatments which we know of, all that remains are fragments, whether of the works themselves or of summaries or short quotations by later writers.

Homer's *Odyssey* provides the fullest, and earliest, account we have of the revenge for Agamemnon's murder. The story is told several times in this epic, each time by a different speaker. The purpose of the multiple accounts is to encourage Telemachus to kill the suitors who are courting his mother and consuming his father's goods while Odysseus is away. Orestes is thus consistently held up as an example of a courageous and loyal son who avenged a wrong done to his father (1.298-300), while Aegisthus is drawn as a villain — a seducer and murderer with no redeeming qualities (*Odyssey* 3.194-98, 256-61, 4.524-37). The murder is described as having been carried out at a homecoming banquet that Aegisthus arranged and is depicted as a sneaky and cowardly ambush. No subsequent pre-dramatic treatment that has come down to us shows Aegisthus in a positive light, and most treatments highlight the element of treachery and deceit in the act.

In the *Odyssey*, we also find the basis for Clytemnestra's depiction as Aegisthus' consort and as a participant in the murder. Her character, motives, and culpability for the murder, however, are presented from different perspectives. Athena, Menelaus, and Agamemnon all describe her as a treacherous woman who took part in the plot to kill her husband (3.234-35, 4.90-92, 11.409-10, 421-35, 454-57). Agamemnon describes her as so pitiless and hard-hearted that she would not even close his eyes after he died. Nestor, on the other hand, depicts her as a woman of "understanding mind" who succumbed to Aegisthus' seductions only after "the doom of the gods bound her so that she must submit." Yet he also tells that she was led to Aegisthus' house "as willing as he [Aegisthus] was" (3.265-72).

Clytemnestra's culpability is more clearly established in later works. Although she is not shown wielding the murder weapon — the first extant intimation of this is in Aeschylus' *Agamemnon* — she is presented as a participant in Agamemnon's murder. We see this first in the seventh-century *Oresteia* written by Stesichorus of Himera in Sicily (640-555 BCE). From the fragments of the poem that have come down to us, we learn that Stesichorus' *Oresteia* described Clytemnestra's dream of Agamemnon's revenge. "She dreamt there came a snake, with bloodstained crest, and out of it there appeared a king of the line of Pleisthenes" (*PMG* 219). This anxiety-ridden dream, related by both Aeschylus (*Libation Bearers* 32-41, 523-53) and Sophocles (*Electra* 417-30), points to Clytemnestra's fear of retribution for her role in the murder.

By the fifth century, Clytemnestra is depicted not only as an active participant in Agamemnon's murder, but also as threatening Orestes' life. Two fifth-century vase paintings show her brandishing an axe in the direction of Orestes, who has just killed Aegisthus.[13] Pindar, in a brief aside in his ode in praise of Thrasydaeus, describes Clytemnestra as a ruthless and treacherous woman from whom Orestes had to be rescued after she killed his father (*Pythian* 11.17-21).

---

13   Red-figure pelike by the Berlin Painter (Vienna, Kunsthistorisches Museum 3725); red-figure stamnos by the Copenhagen Painter (once Berlin F2184, now lost). For the myth in art, see Prag (1985).

At the same time, motives other than lust for Aegisthus also emerge for Clytemnestra's actions. Hints of other motives first appear in two epic poems, the *Cypria* (c. 776 BCE) and the *Nostoi* (c. 750 BCE), which formed part of what later came to be called the *Epic Cycle*. With the exception of a few fragments, all that remains of these poems are short summaries composed in the fifth century CE by Proclus. The *Cypria*, which recounts events that led up to the Trojan war, related Agamemnon's sacrifice of Iphigenia, which was not recounted in Homer. Although the *Cypria* version differs significantly from that adopted in the three revenge plays, the story implicitly raised the possibility that Clytemnestra's motive for killing Agamemnon was not lust, but vengeance for her daughter's murder. The *Nostoi,* which recounts the heroes' return from Troy, tells that Agamemnon brought Cassandra home as a concubine. This allows jealousy as a motive.

Both these possibilities are available in Pindar's ode to Thrasydaeus. The ode does not specifically name jealousy as a motive, but does tell that Clytemnestra killed Cassandra, and questions whether Clytemnestra's motive for killing Agamemnon was lust for Aegisthus or anger at Iphigenia's slaughter (*Pythian* 11.17-28).

Orestes is consistently drawn as the dutiful son who did what he was honor bound to do in avenging his father's murder. Different accounts, however, deal differently with his role as a matricide, a son who killed his own mother. The *Odyssey* clearly tells us that he killed Aegisthus but leaves his role in the killing of his mother vague, even as it relates that Clytemnestra was killed in the episode.[14] The vagueness enables the poet to avoid directly presenting Orestes as a matricide, which could raise questions about his morality and undermine his heroic stature. The only other information given about Orestes in the Homeric works is that he came from Athens and killed his father's murderer thereafter (*Odyssey* 3.306-307).

Orestes' killing of his mother came into sharper focus in subsequent works, in tandem with the heightening of Clytemnestra's culpability. The sixth-century BCE pseudo-Hesiodic *Catalogue of Women* is the first known source that clearly states that Orestes killed not only his father's murderer (Aegisthus) but also his "man-slaying mother" (fr. 23 (a) M-W, 13-30). The *Nostoi* has him killing Aegisthus and Clytemnestra both. So does Pindar (*Pythian* 11.36-37).

The attribution to Clytemnestra of an active role in Agamemnon's death provides a measure of justification for the matricide, as does the depiction of her as threatening Orestes' life. Yet there was apparently need

---

14   Aristarchus, a 2nd century BCE commentator on Homer, maintains that the line shows that she was killed along with Aegisthus, but not necessarily by Orestes.

for even further exculpation. This is provided by the inclusion of Apollo in the treatments of the myth. As Jebb (p.xiii) explains, Apollo, the god of light and all-seeing arbiter of purity, had the power to grade the degree of homicidal guilt and to free persons of the defilement and punishment that ensued from shedding kindred blood. The first known allusion to Apollo, along with Pylades, in connection with the story was in the *Nostoi*, which recounts how Pylades of Phocis helped Orestes kill his father's murderers. Stesichorus of Himera has Apollo giving Orestes a bow to fend off the Erinyes, or Furies, the primitive powers that punished the murder of kin.

Electra comes into the myth relatively late. The *Iliad* names three daughters of Agamemnon, the *Cypria* four. Both mention Chrysothemis (who figures in Sophocles' play) and Iphianassa; neither names Electra. The first known reference to Electra is in the now lost *Oresteia* by the seventh-century BCE poet Xanthus, who (according to Aelian) claimed that Electra was Homer's Laodice and that Laodice was given the name *Electra* because she remained so long unmarried: *alektros*. The pseudo-Hesiodic *Catalogue of Women* identifies Electra as the daughter of Clytemnestra and Agamemnon, and Orestes as their son. Stesichorus' *Oresteia*, according to P. Oxy. 2506 (*PMG* 217), mentioned the recognition by the lock of hair. This places Electra firmly in the story of the revenge. We do not know from these sources, however, how her participation was depicted: how active, how passive, and whether commended or criticized.

All three tragedians had the same mythic material to draw on. Yet each placed the action in a different setting, depicted the characters and their interactions in a different way, and turned the material to his own themes and purposes.

The Three Playwrights:
The Dilemma of Matricidal Revenge

The matricidal revenge of Agamemnon's murder is the only Greek myth for which we have extant treatments by all three great Athenian playwrights of the fifth century BCE. Aeschylus produced the *Libation Bearers* (*Choephoroi*) in 458. Sophocles' *Electra* is dated between 418 and 410, Euripides' *Electra* between 415 and 413. Scholars still dispute which *Electra* was produced first.

Of the three playwrights, Aeschylus is the only one who treated the entire sweep of the myth in a trilogy. The *Libation Bearers*, which dramatizes the revenge, is the middle play, lodged between the *Agamemnon*, which dramatizes Clytemnestra's murder of Agamemnon, and the *Eumenides*, which shows Orestes pursued by the Furies (the archaic goddesses who punish kindred murder), his trial for matricide, and his acquittal through the intervention of Athena. Thus placed, the matricidal revenge comes across as the inevitable consequence of Clytemnestra's treacherous murder, which, in turn, was presented as the unavoidable consequence of Agamemnon's sacrifice of Iphigenia.

Sophocles and Euripides both restrict themselves to a single play, which dramatizes the revenge but, of necessity, treats its antecedents most briefly and its aftermath either briefly (Euripides) or not at all (Sophocles). In both cases, this paring down has the effect of reducing the sense of inevitability that pervades Aeschylus' trilogy and enables the playwrights to highlight the role of the characters themselves — rather than of the situation or of the workings of the ancient curse — in the matricide.

In addition, both Sophocles and Euripides shift Aeschylus' focus from Orestes, who is the hero of both the *Libation Bearers* and the *Eumenides*, to Electra, their plays' namesake. In the *Libation Bearers*, Electra is a secondary figure. She enters at the beginning of the play, bearing her mother's libations for Agamemnon's grave, and exits shortly after the midpoint, not to return again. She never appears alone. Her main function is to set the stage for Orestes' long awaited arrival and retaliation. Orestes commits the matricide and suffers its consequences on his own.

In both Sophocles' and Euripides' plays, Electra is the main character. She remains on stage throughout most of the action. She is also more complex than Aeschylus' heroine. Like Aeschylus' Electra, Sophocles' and Euripides' heroines too suffer from the loss of their father, hate his murderers, and eagerly await Orestes' return to wreak vengeance on them. Sophocles depicts his Electra as absorbed by grief and emphasizes her deprivations and servitude in the home of the royal couple. Euripides casts his heroine as forcibly married to a poor peasant farmer beneath her in station and deprived of the amenities due her royal status. At the same time, both playwrights subtly undermine the unadulterated sympathy that Aeschylus bestows on his heroine. Aeschylus' Electra is a young, pure, innocent, and passive figure. Their Electras are older; their appeal as women who have been wronged is marred by their bitterness, anger, and stubbornness; and their innocence is undermined by the fact that they are present during the killing and take an active role in it. Moreover, in making Electra the heroine and relegating Orestes to a secondary role, Sophocles and Euripides undercut the heroism of revenge —presenting it as an act driven by women.

A further difference is in the playwrights' treatment of the dilemma raised by the myth. What made the story so compelling for the ancient Greeks was the collision of two strongly held moral injunctions: the injunction that sons avenge wrongs to their fathers and the injunction against killing a parent. Had the revenge begun and ended with the killing of Aegisthus, it would have been unproblematic and of little dramatic interest. In the moral code of the day, it would have been entirely right and proper for Orestes to kill the man who had stolen his father's wife, usurped his father's throne, taken his father's life, and robbed him of his patrimony, and for Electra to support him. They would have been remiss had they behaved differently.

The killing of Clytemnestra was another matter entirely. Matricide, killing the person who gave one life, is an instinctively heinous act, which violates the most basic of human ties and obligations. In doing right by their father, Orestes and Electra thus had to act toward their mother in a way that no society can sanction, but which was nonetheless required of them.

Aeschylus deals with this dilemma by crafting his trilogy to justify Orestes' killing of his mother. The *Agamemnon* depicts Clytemnestra as a treacherous wife who welcomes Agamemnon back from the Trojan War with professions of admiration and love only to murder him shortly afterward. To underscore the heinousness of her act, the play treats the audience to Cassandra's vivid description of the murder as it is committed behind the palace walls and then shows Clytemnestra gloating over the dead bodies of her husband and Cassandra. It allows Clytemnestra her motives, by giving a great deal of space to the sacrifice of Iphigenia and by showing Agamemnon bringing home a concubine. Nonetheless, the play ends by showing her and Aegisthus as incipient tyrants who will deprive the Argive people of their liberty — the implication being that it is right and necessary to stop them. The *Libation Bearers* continues the justification by stripping Clytemnestra of the sympathy she was allowed in the *Agamemnon*. It highlights Agamemnon's greatness, makes no mention of Clytemnestra's motives, and emphasizes her evil by repeated and gruesome descriptions of the murder, and by depicting her as ready to kill Orestes as well. In addition, it has both the Chorus and the gods throw their support strongly and unequivocally behind the vengeance. The *Eumenides*, which deals with the emotional repercussions of the matricide, completes the justification. At the end of the *Libation Bearers* Orestes is driven from the palace by the Furies, representative of the agonies of conscience suffered by the matricide, however right and justified the deed is. In the *Eumenides*, Aeschylus has Orestes purified by Apollo, who had commanded the murder, and exculpated by Athena, who casts the decisive vote in his trial before the court of the Aeropagus. This court, which takes into consideration the motives and circumstances of a crime, replaces the archaic Furies, who are banished to a deep chamber of the underworld, while the court becomes the arbiter of right and wrong.[15] Thus, even as Orestes suffers terrible pangs of conscience for his matricide, he is vindicated in the end.

Aeschylus' endorsement of the matricide reflects the Athenian view in the first half of the fifth century that revenge was the solution to a wrong done to one, not the problem. As Burnett (xvi, 225-226) describes it, this view gradually lost its attractiveness in the wake of the protracted Peloponnesian War (431-404 BCE) and the ensuing political strife. Retaliation became an everyday event that provoked fear and threatened civic order. By the end of the century, it had begun to lose its appeal. Against this background, neither Euripides' nor Sophocles' play justifies the matricide.

Euripides' *Electra* condemns it. His play follows Aeschylus in treating the revenge as the inevitable outcome of the crimes that had preceded it, but casts a skeptical eye on the matricide. Orestes has qualms from the very beginning and even questions the reliability of the oracle that commanded it. Electra is shown as the chief instigator, as she goads her brother to commit the act with accusations of cowardice (982), and plots it herself. The play intimates that had she not been married off to a poor farmer but allowed to enjoy the good life of the palace, she would have been less filled with indignation at her mother. She is shown exploiting her mother's kindness and maternal feelings to lure her to her death. Immediately after the matricide, the Chorus, who had solidly supported the murder of Aegisthus, turn against the perpetrators. Even as they acknowledge Clytemnestra's crimes and the justice of her punishment, they criticize Electra's judgment (1202-205) and decry the act as an "interchange of evils" (1147). At the end of the play, Clytemnestra's deceased brothers are brought onto the scene as *dei ex machina* to declare "She got her justice, but you have not worked in justice" (1244) and to confirm Orestes' suspicion that Apollo's oracles were misleading or incorrect (1246). The play's final judgment is that the matricide was a wicked act orchestrated by a headstrong and embittered woman under the misapprehension that it was the divine will.

Sophocles' position is less clear. His Chorus repeatedly warn Electra of the disastrous consequences of her wallowing in grief and of opposing the royal couple, yet with equal consistency remind us of their misdeeds and endorse the vengeance. His Orestes and Electra are free of inner conflict, never waver in their certainty of its morality, and express no qualms about the matricide, even after it is completed. Yet, we do not find in Sophocles' play the explicit justification of the matricide that runs through Aeschylus' trilogy, and both Orestes and Electra have qualities of character — Orestes'

---

15   For the court's decision, see Roisman (1987).

marked rationality and practicality, Electra's self-destructive hatred and grief — that might raise questions about the rightness of their deeds.

Not surprisingly, scholars are sharply divided on the play's attitude toward vengeance in general and the matricide in particular. At one extremity, Jebb (1894) claims that Sophocles adopted the epic position that Orestes' deed was entirely laudable. Woodard (1966) views the action of the play as leading to the triumph of good. Burnett (1998) sees the revenge as a cleansing of the pollution wrought by the murder of Agamemnon. March (2001), reviving many of Jebb's points, argues that the play presents the vengeance as an unqualified act of justice, approved by the gods. At the other extreme, Sheppard (1927, 2-9), in a defense of Sophocles' "morality," argues that Sophocles subtly lets us know that Apollo never actually sanctioned the vengeance and that Orestes carried it out of his own accord. Kells (1973) contends that Sophocles makes the matricide abhorrent and repellent. The scholars on the two sides of the divide differ too on practically every other issue in the play, from Electra's and Orestes' characters through the tenor of the play's ending.

Yet, contradictory as they are, neither set of readings can be readily dismissed, as the play lends itself to both. Thus, a good number of scholars have suggested that such either/or readings are inadequate. Segal (1966) observes that Sophocles' *Electra* is a play in which "the ground shifts from under our feet from scene to scene" (473). Schein (1982) describes it as a "deliberately confusing problem play" (79). Buxton (1984, 29) notes that: "It would seem *Electra* is a play in which the significance of the ending may legitimately be molded by a director in either a positive or negative sense without his being false to the text." Hartigan (1996) states that the play is "shrouded in ambiguity" (83). Winnington-Ingram (1980) observes most informatively that Sophocles presents both the vengeance and the absence of vengeance as problematic, since "in the tragic circumstances, there is no mode of conduct which can be truly salutary and truly laudable" (246).

On the Translation

In translating Sophocles' *Electra*, I relied on Pearson's and Lloyd-Jones and Wilson's Greek texts. My aim was to offer an accessible translation as close as possible to the sense of the Greek. Sophocles' wonderful poetry was necessarily sacrificed in the process.

A major question that confronts translators of Greek is how consistent to be in rendering the same Greek word in English. Ancient Greek is a polysemous language, in which a single word can have a wide range of meanings depending on the context. Always translating the same Greek word by the same English word has the advantages of highlighting repeated motifs and of enabling comparison, whether between characters as they use the same words or when the same character uses the same word in different situations. On the other hand, such consistency has many pitfalls. While ancient Greek audiences probably grasped the appropriate denotation at each point where a polysemous word was used, modern English readers would not be able to.

Like most modern translators, I adopted both approaches. For example, the Greek *dolos* can be translated as "trickery," "guile," "cunning," "stealth," and so on, or "treachery." In three out of its four appearances in the text, I translated it as "guile" to highlight this theme in the play. In line 279, however, I used the adverb "treacherously" both because it seems more natural and to underscore Clytemnestra's betrayal of Agamemnon. For the Greek adjective *kakos*, I took a looser approach. This word, which appears thirty-nine times in the text (as an adjective, adverb or noun), refers to many forms of bad or evil and of sorrow or suffering. I translated it in nineteen ways: sorrow(s), suffering(s), disasters, evil(s), miseries, disloyal, calamity, trouble(s), wicked, hardships, incident, misfortune, failing, afflictions, abomination, mistreatment, perils, ruinous, and tribulations.

Other questions concern how to handle the many self-expressions of suffering and misery in the play. One case in point is the adjective *talas, talaina*, which is variously translated as "suffering," "wretched," "sad," "miserable," and "sorry," as well as "enduring," "foolhardy," and "headstrong." It appears twenty-one times in the play and is applied to every character except the Paedagogus. The main problem is that Electra applies it ten times to herself. In ancient Greek tragedy, it was perfectly acceptable for a character to say of herself, "poor me," "wretched me," "miserable me." In English, such talk sounds contrived and self-pitying. Without removing the self-referential use of the term from the translation altogether, there is no way of solving this problem.

Another instance is the extensive use of a variety of shrieks and cries in Greek tragedy. *Electra* uses nine: *O!; io; e, e, io!; pheu!; oimoi!; oimoi moi; omoi; aiai; e, e, aiai!; papai!*. These ejaculations enabled the playwright to convey emotion, which could not be conveyed by facial expression because of the actors' masks or by subtle gestures, which would not have been visible to most of the spectators in the large amphitheatre. Here, too, in English the *oh's* and *ah's* by which these ejaculations are conventionally translated sound self-pitying, overwrought, and artificial. Where the meaning is adequately conveyed without them, I generally eliminated them.

I removed many of the conjunctions from the text. Greek uses conjunctions far more abundantly than English, where semantic linkage is easily understood from the sequence.

Names are transliterated using the most common English renditions.

SOPHOCLES: *ELECTRA*

SPEAKING CHARACTERS:

Orestes son of Agamemnon and Clytemnestra, arrived in Argos to avenge his father's murder.

Electra grieving daughter of the murdered Agamemnon, the former king of Mycenae, and Clytemnestra.

Chrysothemis Electra's sister, daughter of Agamemnon and Clytemnestra.

Paedagogus The word refers to a personal slave who took young boys to their teachers. Here the Paedagogus is the elderly slave who smuggled Orestes to Phocis when Agamemnon was murdered and who has now brought him back to his homeland. He has more standing and authority with Orestes than we today associate with slaves.

Clytemnestra Agamemnon's wife, who together with her lover, Aegisthus, murdered Agamemnon on his return from Troy. She now rules Argos along with Aegisthus.

Aegisthus Agamemnon's cousin, who, with Clytemnestra, murdered Agamemnon. Now he rules Argos with her.

SILENT CHARACTERS

Pylades Son of Strophius, King of Crisa in Phocis, and of Anaxibia, Agamemnon's sister. Orestes was raised with Pylades in Strophius' court.

Maidservant to Clytemnestra

Attendants of Orestes and Pylades

---

* When a line is split among two or more speakers, except for the first speaker their words are indented.

The Paedagogus, Orestes, and Pylades enter by a side entrance (eisodos) on the left of the spectators. They stand in front of the central door of the stage-building, which represents the palace of the Pelopids in Mycenae. It is early morning. A statue of Apollo stands near the palace.

Paedagogus

Son of Agamemnon, who once commanded the
troops at Troy, now you can cast your eyes
on the sights you've always yearned to see.
For this is the ancient Argos for which you've longed.
Here, the sacred grove of the gadfly-stung daughter of Inachus.   5
And this, Orestes, is the Lycean marketplace
of the wolf-slaying god; and here to the left, the
famous temple of Hera; and from here
you can say you see Mycenae, wrought in gold,
and the palace of Pelops' sons, plagued by disasters.   10
From there, after your father's murder,
I took you from your sister, your flesh and blood,
carried you and saved you and raised you from childhood
to your young manhood to avenge your father's murder.

1-2   Although it was customary to introduce characters by their patronymic, in doing so at the very opening of the play and in highlighting Agamemnon's military identity, Sophocles leads the audience to expect that Orestes, too, will act heroically.

2-10   This verbal scene painting, coming in place of elaborate stage props, tells us that Orestes, Pylades, and the Paedagogus are standing in front of Pelops' sons' palace in Mycenae and draws the surroundings—the grove, market, and temple of Hera—for the audience to envision in their mind's eye.

5   *the gadfly-stung daughter of Inachus*: The Inachus river flows into the plain of Argos from the northwest. Io, Inachus' daughter, was a victim of the love of Zeus and revenge of Hera, who sent a gadfly to sting her continuously.

10   *the palace of Pelops' sons, plagued by disasters*: Pelops' sons are Atreus and Thyestes, respectively the fathers of Agamemnon and Aegisthus, who are thus first cousins. *Plagued by disasters* refers to the murders that took place there before the play's start. Thyestes seduced the wife of Atreus, who was the king of Mycenae. Atreus banished Thyestes, but then recalled him on pretence of being reconciled and prepared a banquet in which he served him the flesh of his two sons. When Thyestes realized the ploy, he fled and called down a curse on the house of Atreus. He fathered Aegisthus by his own daughter. She left the baby out to die, but he was cared for by shepherds. When Atreus learned of the boy's existence he brought him up as his own child. When Aegisthus grew up, Atreus sent him to kill his father, but Thyestes recognized him as his son, and the two contrived the death of Atreus instead.

12   *from your sister, your flesh and blood*: Sophocles seems to highlight right from the beginning the idea of blood relations. See 532.

So now, Orestes, and you, most beloved of hosts,   15
Pylades, the time has come to promptly decide what must be done.
For the sun's bright rays stir up
the birds' clear, early morning songs for us,
and the black and starry night has gone.
So now, before anyone leaves the house,   20
we must confer, because we've reached the point where
it's no longer time for holding back, but high time to act.

Orestes

Dearest of my servants, how clear the signs
you show me of your loyalty.
For just as a well-bred horse, even when old,   25
does not lose his courage in time of danger,
but pricks up his ears, so you too urge me forward
and are among the first to follow my commands.
I will explain my decision.
Give sharp ear to my words, and if I'm   30
off the mark, correct me.
When I came to the Pythian oracle
to learn how to exact
retribution for my father from his murderers,
Phoebus gave me this prophecy, which you will hear right now: 35
that, unfurnished with army or armed men, I use guile
to steal the just slaying with my own hands.

20-22   This is the first of three times in the play that the Paedagogus urges Orestes to get on
    with his revenge. His repeated references to time create a sense of urgency. The word
    kairos signifying the "right time" is used by Orestes in lines 40, 75, 1259, 1368.

23-27   The comparison of the Paedagogus to a horse may be both a sign of regard, as horses
    were considered spirited and intelligent animals, and an assertion of status, since it
    is ultimately the rider, Orestes, who is master.

32-36   The Pythian oracle is the oracle of Apollo, son of Zeus. Sophocles, like Aeschylus
    before him (*Libation Bearers* 269-305, 554-59, 900-902), has Apollo sanction the
    revenge because he is the god who determines whether a murder is justified. In Eurip-
    ides' *Electra*, Orestes *post factum* disputes the right of Apollo to tell him to murder
    his mother. Note that Orestes does not ask Apollo whether to avenge his father's
    death, but how to do so. The rightness and necessity of the revenge are assumed. See
    Introduction 15.

36-37   The use of guile to exact the revenge is common to all three dramatic treatments of
    the story (*Libation Bearers* 554-84; Euripides' *Electra* 635-68). The guile has a cer-
    tain retributive propriety in that Aegishus and Clytemnestra had killed Agamemnon
    using guile. In Aeschylus' *Libation Bearers* (274), Orestes says he was bidden to take
    revenge in the same way as his father had been killed.

Now that we've heard the prophecy,
you must go into the house when
the opportunity arises, find out all that's going on there,   40
and, having found out, bring us a sure report of it.
Given your age and the long time gone by, they won't
recognize you; nor will they suspect you with your hair
now decked out with white. Tell this story: that you're
a stranger come from Phanoteus the Phocian,   45
the greatest of their allies.
Tell them, swearing it's true, that
Orestes died in a fatal accident:
that at the Pythian Games, he was heaved headlong from a chariot
driving at breakneck speed. Let this be the substance of your story. 50
In the meantime, as the god commanded, we'll deck
my father's grave with libations and locks of my
luxuriant hair. Then we'll come back here
carrying in our hands the brass-sided urn,
which, as I believe you know, is hidden in the bushes.   55
And to deceive them with words, we'll bring
them a story, sweet to their ears, that my body
is no more: that it has been burnt and turned to ashes.
For what harm does it do me that I'm dead in
words when I'm still alive and achieve glory in deeds.   60

---

45   Phocis is north of Boeotia, a mountain district in central Greece. Phanoteus was an
      ally of Clytemnestra and Aegisthus and enemy of Strophius' father, Crisis.

49   The Pythian games were held every four years and were second in importance only
      to the Olympian games. The full story of the chariot race is told in lines 680-763.

52   *libations:* For fifth-century Athenians, visiting the graves of relatives was as important
      as attending the internment. By pouring drink offerings of water, wine, milk, oil, or
      honey or some mixture thereof, they would summon the spirit of the deceased to attend
      the rite being enacted in their honor. As here, the libations were generally followed by
      a prayer to the deceased asking for a blessing or a favor. See Garland (2001). From 894
      we learn that Orestes poured milk. Offering a lock of hair on a tomb was customary.
      Orestes does the same in Aeschylus' *Libation Bearers* 6-7, and Euripides' *Electra* 91.

54   Both cremation and burial were used in fifth-century Athens. Some of the upper classes
      preferred cremation, in which case the ashes of the dead were retained in urns, which
      were about eighteen inches high.

56   *to deceive them with words:* The ability of words to deceive is a recurrent theme in
      this (cf. 73-74, 347-350, 357-58) and other plays by Sophocles, and reflects a major
      fifth-century concern.

59-60 This is the first of several contrasts between words and deeds made in the play. Electra
      contrasts them in lines 357-58, 624-25 and 1359-60, and Orestes in 1372-73.

I think that no speech that brings profit is bad.
For I've often seen even clever men
play dead in false reports, and then
honored all the more when they've come home.
So I'm confident that I, too, from this rumor   65
will come out alive and will yet shine like a star above my enemies.
But you, land of my fathers and gods of my country,
receive me with good fortune on this journey,
and you too, my father's house, for I come
with justice, as your purifier, urged on by the gods.   70
And do not send me away from this land dishonored, but
receive me as the master of my wealth and restorer of my home.
This is all I have to say on the matter. But you, old man,
go now and get on with the job.
And we two will be on our way, for it's time, and timing   75
is man's greatest commander in every act.

Electra's voice is heard from inside the palace.

Electra
Poor me, poor unhappy me!

Paedagogus
I think, my son, I hear from behind the doors
a maidservant moaning softly inside.

Orestes
Isn't it the unfortunate Electra? Should   80
we stay here and listen to her cries?

Paedagogus
Not at all! Let's not do anything until we carry out
Apollo's commands, and then let's proceed from there
to pour the lustral offerings for your father. For I say these
actions will bring us victory and the upper hand in our endeavor.   85

---

61   *no speech that brings profit is bad*: This line was included by Cephisidorus, a pupil
      of the orator Isocrates (436-338 BCE), among the ignoble statements to be found in
      the works of great poets (Athenaeus 122c). See Essay 96.

77   *Poor me, poor unhappy me!* The play is full of bursts of emotion and screams, most,
      but not all of them, by Electra. For the screams as part of Electra's characterization
      and the difficulty of translating them, see Carson (1996). See also Introduction 16.

Orestes and Pylades exit by one of the side entrances, the
Paedagogus by the other. Electra comes out of the central door
of the stage building.

Electra

Oh holy light and air,
equal partner of earth!
How many doleful laments,
how many blows beating
my breast till it is bloodied have you heard   90
before the dusky night comes to its end?
In this wretched house,
by now this loathsome bed of mine
knows well my all-night vigils, when
I bemoan my unfortunate father to whom bloody   95
Ares gave no resting place in a foreign land,
but my mother and her bedfellow,
Aegisthus, as woodmen fell an oak,
cleft his skull with a bloody axe.
And for this, I'm the only one to   100
grieve for you, father, who died
so unfitting and so pitiful a death.
But no, I swear
I will not cease my pain-filled lamentations,
as long as I can see the resplendent sweep   105
of the stars and this daylight.
No, but as some nightingale who lost her young,
I shall cry out in lamentation
outside these doors of my father's house.

86-120 Electra comes out of the palace (stage building) after the Paedagogus and Orestes
have left the stage but before the Chorus comes down to the *orchestra*. Although it
is not unusual for a character to address the audience before the Chorus sing, it is
unusual to do so before the Chorus actually arrive. The length and constancy of her
grief contrasts with the Paedagogus' emphasis on the specific opportune time (19-22n)
for the vengeance.

97-98 *Electra* is similar to the *Odyssey*, which, as noted in the Introduction 9, attributes the
murder sometimes to Aegisthus only (*El.* 269-70, 955-57), sometimes to Clytemnestra
(124-26, 278-79, 408, 444-46, 526, 578-79), and sometimes to both (205-6, 263, 358,
587-88, 815-16).

107 The reference to the nightingale here presages the more specific reference to Procne
(147-49n).

Oh house of Hades and Persephone!   110
Oh Hermes of the netherworld and you mighty Curse!
And Furies, holy children of the gods,
who see those who died unjustly,
you who see those cheated in their marriage beds,
come! help me! avenge   115
our father's murder
and send me my brother.
For I no longer have the strength
to bear up under the weight of my grief.   120

The Chorus of women of Mycenae enter by a side entrance.

Chorus   *Strophe*
Electra, child of the most terrible
mother! Why are you forever melting
away like this in such insatiable mourning
for your father Agamemnon?— he who your
deceitful mother trapped most godlessly and who was betrayed   125
by a treacherous hand. May he who has
done this perish, if it is right for me to say so.

---

111   Hermes is the god who conveys the souls of the dead to the Netherworld.

112-13 Furies, also called Erinyes, are the spirits who punish those who commit crimes against
      kin, as well as perjurers and persons who violate the laws of hospitality and the rules
      of supplication. As Aeschylus describes them in the *Eumenides*, their punishments are
      internal torments, inflicted without mercy or consideration for the circumstances or
      causes of the offence. They can thus be thought of as a primal, very harsh conscience.
      At the end of the *Eumenides*, Athena banishes them deep underground and their harsh
      justice is replaced by the justice of the Athenian homicide court of the Aeropagus.

121-235 The Chorus file into the *orchestra* and address Electra with lyric strains, to which
      she responds in lyric measures. The *parodos* thus becomes a *kommos*, an antiphonal
      lyric exchange between the Chorus and the protagonist. In this case, *kommos* is ritual
      lament in which the mourner's words are interspersed with a refrain or cries from the
      women present during the wake. In this lyrical dialogue, the Chorus dance and sing
      in responsive stanzas with Electra, who also sings and dances.

125-26 The ancient literature more often attributes the deception used to trap Agamemnon
      to Clytemnestra (279) than to Aegisthus (See Homer's *Odyssey* 4.92, 11.422, 429,
      24.199; Aeschylus' *Agamemnon* 1495, 1519 and *Libations Bearers* 991; Euripides'
      Electra 9, 983, and Seneca's *Agamemnon* 116-120, 888-89, 925, 1009).

126-27 The Chorus' switch here from Clytemnestra's treachery in 125-26 to Aegisthus is
      surprising. Are they refraining from suggesting too overtly that Clytemnestra be
      killed, as March (2001) and Sommerstein (1997) 201 suggest? Alternatively, might
      the masculine pronoun here, as in English, be a kind of neuter pronoun that includes
      the female as well? Both Jebb (2004) and Kamerbeek (1974) suggest that it refers to
      both authors of the crime.

Electra

Women born of noble parents
you've come to console me in my troubles.   130
I understand what you're saying; it doesn't escape me.
But I don't want to give up lamenting and
wailing for my poor father. You, who reciprocate
every kind of love,
let me wander thus distraught,   135
I beg you!

Chorus   *Antistrophe*

But you will never bring your father
back from the marshy lakes of Hades, where all of us
will have to go, not by your wailing and not by your prayers.
Yet, leaving behind all moderation, you're destroying   140
yourself with constant groaning and
intractable grief. There is no deliverance whatsoever
from your sorrows in this. Why do you yearn
after what is so hard to bear?

Electra

Only a simpleton forgets   145
parents who died piteously.
No! It is that mournful bird that suits my mind,
the bird who is distraught by grief, the messenger of Zeus,
who forever laments Itys! Itys!
Oh, you too, all-suffering,
Niobe, to me you're a goddess,   150

147-49 *that mournful bird*: Procne, the nightingale referred to in line 107. Procne killed her
son Itys and served his flesh to her husband, Tereus, in revenge for his rape and mutilation of her sister Philomela. Turned into a nightingale to escape Tereus' pursuit, she
spent her time ceaselessly singing her son's name in mourning. Cf. 1077. The repeated
reference emphasizes Electra's mourning. Traditionally, Zeus' messenger was the
eagle. Kells (1973) suggests that the nightingale was considered a messenger of Zeus
because its return to Attica heralds the Spring, which is sacred to Zeus, as are all the
seasons. See Essay 100.

150-52 Niobe had six sons and six daughters (or seven and seven) and boasted that she was
superior to Leto, who had only one of each. In revenge, Apollo and Artemis, the son
and daughter of the offended goddess, killed Niobe's children. Emblematic of her
grief, Niobe was turned into a rock on Mount Sipylus in Lydia, with a spring of water
forever flowing down her face like tears. That both the Procne and Niobe myths refer
to a mother's grief for her child rather than to a child's grief for a parent is apparently

you who forever shed tears
in your rocky grave.

Chorus   *Strophe*
Not to you alone
among mortals, child, has grief come,
which you feel more keenly than those indoors,   155
your kin in blood, your sisters Chrysothemis and Iphianassa,
who are alive,
and he who in his youth was hidden away from grief and happy —
he whom one day the illustrious land of Mycenae will receive   160
as heir to his noble father.
With gracious step that comes from Zeus,
he will arrive in this land, Orestes.

Electra
Yes, him I await, tirelessly, endlessly,
living miserably, without a child, without a husband,   165
drenched in tears, with my lot of endless tribulation.
But he forgets what he has suffered
and what he has learned.
For what message comes to me
that doesn't turn out to be a lie?   170
For he's always yearning, yet though yearning
doesn't think it fit to come.

Chorus   *Antistrophe*
Courage, courage,
my child! Still great is

---

lost on Electra, who is focused on their perpetual lamentation. Electra's references
are somewhat ironic in view of the fact that it was Procne herself who killed her son.
See Essay 100.

157-58 Homer gives Agamemnon three daughters: Chrysothemis, Laodice, and Iphianassa
(sometimes identified with Iphigenia). See Introduction 11.

165   Electra seems preoccupied with being unwed and childless, cf. 187-88. Both motifs
are commonplaces of feminine self-pity, cf. *Antigone* 813-14, 867. Women in ancient
Greece married no younger than sixteen and no older than twenty (Plato, *Laws* 785b).
Given that Orestes was spirited away to safety as a child, that Electra is depicted as
his older sister, and that she complains bitterly about being alone and unmarried, we
can deduce that Electra is somewhere in her twenties. According to Homer (*Odyssey*
3.303-306), Aegisthus was killed by Orestes in the eighth year after Agamemnon's
murder, which would make Orestes around eighteen or nineteen.

Zeus above, who watches over and rules everything.   175
To him convey your most anguished wrath,
and neither be overly vexed with those you hate
nor entirely forget them.
Time is an easy god.
For neither Agamemnon's son,   180
this lad who dwells along
the cattle-grazing shore of Crisa,
nor he who rules as a god
alongside Acheron is heedless.

Electra
But for me, much of my life has already gone by   185
without hope, and I have no more strength in me.
I pine away childless,
I have no man near and dear to stand up for me;
but, like an unworthy foreigner,
I tend my father's chambers; and, just   190
as I am, in this unsightly dress,
I stand at empty tables.

Chorus   *Strophe*
Pitiful was the cry on his return,
pitiful in the bedrooms of his fathers,
when the blow of the biting axe   195
made all of brass came down straight at him.

---

182   Crisa, where Orestes has been living, is the home of Strophius, south of Delphi toward the Corinthian gulf.

183-84 *he who rules as a god alongside Acheron*: Most obviously, the "ruler" refers to Hades, the god of the Netherworld. *Acheron*, the River of Woe, is one of the four rivers of the Netherworld. Some scholars see a reference to Agamemnon here. In their view, the Chorus imply that Agamemnon's spirit is powerful in the Netherworld, just as they later sing that Amphiaraus rules in Hades even though he is dead (837-41). However, the reference to Amphiaraus comes too late in the text to be meaningful here. One point of the statement is that it is not Zeus whom the Chorus expect to come to the aid of the avengers.

189-92 The first of several complaints Electra makes of her maltreatment, poor food, and poor clothing (264-65, 354, 452, 597-600, 814-15, 1192-96). Her description accords with her later account to Orestes that she is a slave in her own home (1192).

192   *stand at empty tables* is a resonant image. As Jebb (2004) and Kells (1973) point out, it depicts her standing like a slave or a servant when the rest of royal family recline as they eat. See Essay 99.

It was guile that devised it and lust that murdered.
The two bred terribly a terrible
shape, whether a god or mortal
did the deed.   200

Electra

Oh that day that came, by far the most
hateful day of all to me!
Oh night! Oh abominable horror
of that unspeakable banquet!
My father saw his awful   205
death dealt him by the same two hands
that betrayed and stole my life
from me, that destroyed me.
May the god, the great Olympian,
give them suffering in requital,   210
and may they who have committed such deeds
never enjoy their pomp.

Chorus   *Antistrophe*

Watch yourself! Speak no more!
Don't you understand what sort of words and
deeds got you into your present situation? Do you plunge so   215
unsuitably into disasters of your own making?
You've brought a good portion of your
suffering on yourself by constantly breeding wars
with your disaffected soul. But such contests
cannot be waged with the powerful.   220

Electra

Dreadful deeds forced me to dreadful deeds.
My passion doesn't escape me.
No! But with such dreadful deeds around me,
I will not restrain my disastrous ways

---

218   *constantly breeding wars:* The image of "breeding" carries a bitter irony in view of
       Electra's repeated complaints about her childlessness.

224   *disastrous ways:* translates the Greek *atê*, which has a range of meanings, including
       lack of judgment and its variants (e.g., folly, madness, obsession, delusion, infatua-
       tion); the disaster or catastrophe that results from the lack of judgment; and the divine
       force that drives one to foolish, catastrophic behavior. See Roisman (1983), (1984),
       (1985).

as long as there's life in me.   225
For, my dear ladies, what person
whose wisdom is attuned to the moment
can give me useful advice?
Leave me, leave me, you who try to console me.
There's no resolution to my suffering,   230
and I'll never cease my labors
and infinite laments.

Chorus   *Epode*
I speak like a loyal mother,
wishing only your good, imploring you not to
keep breeding disaster from disasters.   235

Electra
Tell me, then, what limit is there to evil?
How can it be good to neglect the dead?
To what human being is this natural?
May I never be honored among such people
nor live complacently with   240
whatever good may come my way if
I clip the sharp-voiced wings
of my laments so they leave my
father without honor.
For if he who is dead, lying there wretchedly,   245

---

227   *to the moment:* Electra despairs of finding anyone who has a sense of the hour, of what she needs at this moment. She doesn't believe that anyone can say anything that could be of solace to her. Both siblings are aware of the importance of the right moment.

234-35 *not to keep breeding disaster from disasters:* The Chorus emphasize the idea that Electra generates her own destruction (217-19).

236   *what limit is there to evil?* The question is an angry response to the Chorus' criticism of Electra's unbounded mourning. The line allows several rather different readings. Some commentators read the word translated here as "evil" as sorrow, others as evil /wickedness. Moreover, given that Greek does not usually specify possessive pronouns, the word can refer to the concept, in which case Electra would be asking a general philosophical question, or a question more specific to Electra's ("my") sorrow or to the royal couple's ("their") evil — in which case Electra's question would be either self-pitying or a critical statement about the royal couple. The Greek would have allowed for all these understandings simultaneously, and it is likely that Sophocles exploited the richness of possibilities here.

244   *father:* Although *goneôn* is plural in Greek, most modern translators (Jebb [2004], Grene [1991], March [2001]) render the word as the singular "father." Kells (1973) states: "she speaks of 'parents', though only one is concerned."

is earth and nothing,
and they do not repay
the just recompense for their murder,
then shame and respect for law
will forsake all mortals.   250

Chorus
It's in both your interest
and mine that I came, but if I don't speak rightly,
be it as you wish; we will follow you.

Electra
I'm ashamed, ladies, if I seem to you
to grieve too much with my many lamentations.   255
But unlawful force compels me to this.
Forgive me. But how can any well-born woman
not act this way when she sees the sufferings of her
father's house, as I see them, grow and flourish rather
than whither, day by day and night by night?   260
First, things with my mother, who gave me birth,
turned rancorous; then, in my
own house I live with my father's murderers.
I'm ruled by them, and it's up to them
whether I get the things I need or not.   265
What do you think my days are like
when I see Aegisthus sitting on my father's throne?
and when I look at him wearing the same
clothes my father wore and pouring libations
at the very hearth where he killed him?   270
and when I see the ultimate outrage:
the murderer in my father's bed
with my wretched mother, if one can

249-50 *then shame and respect for law will forsake all mortals:* Shame, which the Greeks
viewed as an emotion that kept people from doing wrong, will be lost if people stop
caring whether or not justice has been done to the dead. For a recent study of the
concept of shame in ancient Greece, see Cairns (1993) esp. 247-248.

270   The hearth was the most sacred place in the house, where the head of the household
poured the ritual libations at the end of the evening meal and at sacrifices and feasts.

271-73 Electra's frequent references to her mother's sexual betrayal (97-98, 492-94, 561-62,
587-89) contrast with her own asexual existence. Aeschylus' Orestes also charges his
mother with infidelity (*Libation Bearers*, 894-907).

call her a mother, she who sleeps with him?
But she's so reckless that she lives with   275
the polluter, fearing no Furies.
Just the opposite. As if exulting in what she's done,
she singles out the very day she
treacherously slew my father,
and on that day she organizes choral songs and dances and kills   280
sheep as a monthly sacrifice to the gods who preserved her.
While I, at home, ill-fated, weep and melt away,
and cry over this most wretched banquet,
which has been named after him,
all by myself and to myself; for I'm not   285
even allowed to weep my heart's fill.
For this so-called well-born woman speaks to me
with such words and bitter reproaches:
'You godless, hateful creature! Are you the only one
who's lost a father? Do no other people grieve?   290
May you perish miserably! And may
the gods below never free you from your wailing!'
So outrageously she upbraids me, except when she hears
from someone that Orestes is on his way. Then she
comes over to me and shouts insanely: 'Aren't you the cause   295
of this? Isn't this your doing? You, who stole Orestes from
my very arms and smuggled him away!
Know that you'll certainly pay for this as you deserve!'
So she barks. And her illustrious bridegroom,
always at her side, eggs her on her in her abuse.   300
This man, useless in every respect, this total miscreant,
who fights his battles with the aid of women.

---

277   *exulting:* Literally, laughing. Laughter in this play is often an expression of triumphal
       gloating over an enemy. See 807, 1153, 1295, and 1300.

280   Monthly celebrations were frequent in Greece. Agamemnon, like many other Greek
       heroes, had a hero cult, which included a festival. As Hogan (1991) points out, 277-80,
       Sophocles, in an act of "ironic inversion," has made Electra attribute the establishment
       of the cult, and the festival that came with it, "to the hero's murderer."

299   *barks:* The description of Clytemnestra as howling links her to her sister Helen, who,
       in the *Iliad*, refers to herself as a "dog" or "dog-faced" (e.g. 3.180).

302   In Aeschylus' *Agamemnon* (1625) the Chorus address Aegisthus: "Oh you woman!"
       Cf. *Libation Bearers* 304-305.

And I, still waiting for Orestes to come
and put an end to all of this, waste away miserably.
For by always being about to do something, he's destroyed   305
the hopes I had and those I don't dare have.
When things are like this, my friends, it's
impossible to be moderate or pious, but in evil straits
one's conduct must be evil too.

Chorus
Tell me, are you saying all this with   310
Aegisthus nearby, or is he away from home?

Electra
Of course he's gone. Don't think I'd have ventured outside
if he were close by. But, as a matter of fact, he's off in the fields now.

Chorus
I too might have more courage
to talk with you if this is so.   315

Electra
Well, since he's away, ask me what you'd like to know.

Chorus
Well then, I'm asking you: What do you say about your brother?
Is he coming or is he putting it off? I'd like to know.

Electra
He says he's coming, but though he says so, he does nothing of what
    he says.

Chorus
When a man is engaged in a great undertaking, he tends to hesitate. 320

Electra
Well, you can be sure that I didn't save his life by hesitating.

Chorus
Take heart! He's noble of nature, so he'll help his loved ones.

310-16 The lines indicate not only that Electra is a prisoner in the palace when Aegisthus is
      present, but also that Aegisthus, not Clytemnestra, is the one to be feared.

322   *his loved ones:* translation of the Greek *philoi*, which refers to kin and close friends.
      The Chorus' assurance here is ironic in that Orestes' standing by his father and sister
      will entail killing his mother, another kin.

Electra

I believe it. I can assure you that otherwise I wouldn't have lived this
   long.

Chorus

Don't say another word! I see your sister coming out
of the house, Chrysothemis, born of the same father   325
and mother. In her hands she's carrying offerings
like the ones prepared for those underground.

   Enter Chrysothemis from the palace carrying burial offerings.

Chrysothemis

What are you going on about
yet again, having come outside.
After so long, don't you even want to learn   330
not to indulge your foolish anger?
And yet, this I know about myself, that
the present state of affairs pains me, so that if
I had the strength, I'd show them what I think of them.
But as things are now, I think it best to sail with lowered sail,   335
and not do anything that makes them think I mean them harm,
but is bound to fail. And I wish you'd do the very same,
even though justice isn't in the course I recommend,
but in the course you've chosen. But if I'm to live
a free person, I must heed those in power in everything.   340

324-27 Chrysothemis, who serves as Electra's foil in the play, is carrying burial offerings:
   libations (406, 434) and gifts (433) that could have included flowers, fruit, cakes,
   and ornaments. For Sophocles' use of foils to the protagonists, see Kirkwood (1994)
   passim.

328-29 In rebuking her sister for having gone outside, Chrysothemis relies on the view in
   ancient Greece that women's proper place was indoors, men's outdoors. The only
   circumstances in which it was considered proper for well-bred women to be outdoors
   were ritual occasions, such as sacrifices. Later, in 516, Clytemnestra will make much
   the same point. Electra's long presence outside in this play may suggest a certain
   masculinity in her character. Alternatively, her lamentations for her father may be
   viewed as a ritual that justifies her being outside. Clytemnestra's rebuke recalls Electra's
   statement to the Chorus that she wouldn't be outside if Aegisthus were in the vicinity
   (312-13).

335   The Athenians were a seafaring people and their literature abounds in nautical imagery,
   see 1075, *Antigone* 715-17, Euripides, *Medea* 523-25.

Electra

It's terrible that you, your father's daughter, have
completely forgotten him and are concerned only with your mother.
For all your advice to me is learned
from her; you say nothing of your own.
Now choose one or the other: either think wrongly   345
or, thinking rightly, forget your nearest and dearest.
You, who just now said that if you had the
strength you'd show your hatred of them, when I try
to do all I can to avenge our father, you don't join
with me, but try to dissuade me from what I'm doing.   350
Doesn't this conduct add cowardice to our miseries?
For tell me, or learn from me, what would I
gain by stopping my wailing? Am I not alive?
True, wretchedly, I know, but well enough for me.
I nettle them so as to confer honor on the dead —   355
if there's any pleasure where the dead are.
You, who would like us to believe you hate them, your hatred is
in words only; in your deeds you side with your father's murderers.
Well I'll never yield to them, not even if one of them
cared to bestow on me the privileges in which   360
you now revel. May you have a sumptuous table,
and may your life overflow with abundance.
As for me, may my only food be that I don't upset myself;
I don't want any of your privileges. Nor would you
if you were temperate. But as things are, though you could   365
have been called the daughter of the noblest of fathers,
you're called your mother's daughter. You'll look
disloyal to most people if you betray your dead father and your kin.

345-46 Electra ignores Chrysothemis' attempt to flatter her by acknowledging the morality
of her position (338-39) and demands that she take a clear stand. The choice she offers
her, however, is based on the assumption that she will continue to obey the rulers,
as she's been doing all along. It is actually a choice of consciousness. She can obey
them thinking wrongly — that is, wrongly believing that this is the right thing to do.
Or she can obey them thinking rightly—realizing that her compliance is a violation
of her duty to remember her loved ones.

359-62 Electra's repeated reference to Chrysothemis' good food and luxurious clothing (e.g.,
189-92) may indicate how badly she misses these things.

Chorus

By the gods, don't be angry! There's profit to be
had in both your words. If you, Electra, would   370
make use of hers and she, in turn, of yours.

Chrysothemis

For my part, women, I'm pretty well accustomed to
her talk; and I'd never have mentioned this
had I not heard about the terrible calamity coming her way,
which will keep her from her unending lamentations.   375

Electra

Come on now, tell me what this terrible thing is. If you tell
me something worse than my present lot, I'll never argue with you
again.

Chrysothemis

Well, I'll tell you all I know.
If you don't stop your lamentations, they intend
to send you to where you'll never see   380
sunlight again and where you'll tell your troubles over and over
living in a vault beyond the borders of this land.
Think about this, and don't blame me later when you
suffer. For now's the time to use your head.

Electra

Have they really decided to do this to me?   385

Chrysothemis

Yes, as soon as Aegisthus gets back home.

Electra

So let him come as soon as he can, if this is what he wants to do.

Chrysothemis

You headstrong girl! What curses are you bringing down on yourself?

380-82 The threat recalls Antigone's living tomb (*Antigone* 773-74, 885-86, 888, 891-92),
though here there is no explicit indication that Electra will also be starved to death.
For the claim that Sophocles recycled some of the themes of his earlier play *Antigone*
in the *Electra*, see Ringer (1996) 95.

385-414 *Stichomythia*, a rapid exchange of one- or two-liners, is a common device in Greek
tragedy to convey emotional agitation.

Electra

That he should come if he means to do any of these things.

Chrysothemis

So that what may happen to you? What on earth are you thinking?   390

Electra

To escape as far as possible from you people.

Chrysothemis

Don't you care about the life you still have?

Electra

Oh, yes, my life is a marvel of beauty!

Chrysothemis

It could have been, if you knew how to be sensible.

Electra

Don't teach me how to be disloyal to my own.   395

Chrysothemis

That's not what I'm teaching — but to yield to those in power.

Electra

You fawn on them! The course you speak of isn't mine.

Chrysothemis

Yes, but it's mindless to come to grief through folly.

Electra

I'll come to grief, if I must, avenging my father.

Chrysothemis

But our father will pardon this, I know it.   400

Electra

Cowards approve such words.

Chrysothemis

So you won't listen to me or go along with me?

Electra

Of course not! May I never do anything so pointless.

Chrysothemis

Well, then, I'll be on my way to where I was sent.

Electra

Where are you going? Whom are you carrying these offerings for? 405

Chrysothemis

Our mother sent me to pour libations on father's grave.

Electra

What did you say? Libations for her greatest enemy of all mortals?

Chrysothemis

For the man she murdered. Isn't this what you want to say?

Electra

Which of her friends urged her to do this? Whom will she please by this?

Chrysothemis

I think it was because of some nighttime terror.   410

Electra

Gods of my father, come to my aid now at long last!

Chrysothemis

This fear of hers reassures you?

Electra

If you can tell me her dream, I might be able to answer.

Chrysothemis

But I don't know it and can tell you only a little.

Electra

Tell me this little if nothing more! Often in the past,   415
a few words drove mortals to consternation or raised them up.

Chrysothemis

The word is that she saw your father
— and mine — come back to life,
once again at her side. And then he took

405-16 Electra notices that Chrysothemis is carrying libation offerings only after Chrysothemis has stopped trying to persuade her to cease her lamentations and to adopt a
more conciliatory course. That it has taken Electra so long to comment highlights the
single-mindedness of her preoccupation with her father's murder. Having the sisters
turn their attention to the libation offerings enables Sophocles to get around the impasse
in their debate about how to proceed with regard to the royal couple.

419-23 The phallic quality of the staff makes it plain that Orestes is the leafy shoot that, as
Kells (1973) explains, "will overthrow Clytemnestra and Aegisthus and establish his
own dominion in Mycenae." In the *Libation Bearers* (527-33) Clytemnestra dreams that
she gives birth to a snake, which, when she nurses it, draws her blood along with her
milk.

the scepter that he always used to carry   420
– which Aegisthus carries now – and planted it
next to the hearth. And from it a leafy shoot sprouted,
overshadowing all the land of the Myceneans.
This is what I heard told in detail by someone
who was there when she related it to Helios.   425
I don't know any more than this, except that
it's because of her fear that she's sent me.
So I implore you, by our family gods, please listen to me
and don't come to grief through thoughtlessness. For if you repulse me
now, you'll search for me later when you get into trouble again.   430

Electra
No, my dear one! Don't place what you're
carrying in your hands on the grave. For neither custom
nor piety permits you to dedicate funeral honors
or to bring libations from a hate-filled wife to our father.
Rather throw them to the wind or hide them deep in   435
the ground, where nothing of them will reach our
father's place of rest. Let them be kept safe
for her down below, a treasure when her time comes to die.
For if she weren't the most shameless of women,

428-30 Although most editors accept these lines as genuine, some regard them as a later
interpolation, arguing that they are redundant and unconnected with Chrysothemis'
previous statements. However, the lines are quite consistent with Chrysothemis'
earlier warnings (328-31, 335-37, 379-84) and follow logically upon the implication
of Clytemnestra's dream that the queen is disconcerted and that things may be looking up for Agamemnon's children. Chrysothemis is suggesting that Electra would do
better to let things take their course than to act precipitously.

431-34 Electra viewed the libations as impious because Clytemnestra, who sent them, was
polluted after having mutilated Agamemnon's corpse and smeared his blood on his
head. Hogan (1991) argues that if sending libations were considered impious under
the circumstances, Clytemnestra would not have done it, for fear of the gods. In any
case, her motive in sending libations is clearly her fear following her inauspicious
dream.

431-63 This speech is filled with references to enmity and enemies. Clytemnestra's libations
are "hostile" (440-41); Clytemnestra killed Agamemnon in the way one kills an
enemy (444-46) in war; and Electra instructs Chrysothemis to pray that their father
help them against their foes and that Orestes trample their foes under foot (454, 456).
The Greek term that is translated "foes" in these lines (454, 456) denotes personal
enmity, as opposed to the more impersonal hostility of an enemy in war. This is also
the term Electra uses in 594, 980, and 1153, Orestes in 66 and 1295, Clytemnestra in
647, and the Chorus in 1090, though it is variously translated.

she wouldn't be offering hostile   440
libations to honor the man she murdered.
Think: would the dead man receive these
honors on his grave with kindly feelings toward the woman
by whose hand he died like an enemy — without honor,
his corpse mutilated — and who, to cleanse herself, wiped off the 445
bloodstains on his head? You don't think that bringing
these offerings will absolve her of murder, do you?
It can't be! No, throw it all away!
Instead, cut beautiful locks from your hair,
and from me, poor thing that I am, give him these   450
small gifts — but all I have — this dull hair
and my sash, unadorned with embellishments.
Kneel and pray that he come to us from
below the earth as a kindly helper against our foes,
and that his son Orestes live to gain the upper   455
hand and trample under foot his father's foes,
so that in time to come we can deck his graveside with hands
richer than those with which we bear gifts to him today.
I believe, I really believe, that it was he who
took care to send her fearsome dreams.   460
But all the same, do this service to help
yourself and me and the dearest of all men,
the father of us both, who lies in Hades.

Chorus

The girl speaks out of reverence. And you, my dear,
if you have good sense, will do as she says.   465

444-45 The description refers to the rite of *maschalismos*, the treatment of slaughtered
enemies, whose extremities were hacked off and hung around their necks and under
their armpits so as to prevent them from moving and thereby taking vengeance on the
murderer. The Chorus of Aeschylus' *Libation Bearers* (439-43) similarly relate that
Clytemnestra mutilated Agamemnon's corpse.

445-46 Ordinarily, purification was accomplished by sacrificing a pig and washing one's
hands in its blood. Electra's account of her mother's wiping Agamemnon's blood on
his head seems to refer to the ritual, noted by Russo (1992, on *Odyssey* 19.92), whereby
"wiping blood from a sacrificial knife on to the victim was a means of transferring
the guilt to the victim."

Chrysothemis

I certainly will. When something is just, it makes no sense
for two people to argue about it instead of hurrying to do it.
But, friends, if I'm to try to do any of these
things, you, by the gods, must keep mum.
For if my mother hears of this, I expect   470
the time will come when I bitterly regret my audacity.

*Chrysothemis exits by a side entrance still carrying the
libations, which, as the audience understands, she will get rid of
before she reaches her father's tomb.*

Chorus   *Strophe*

If I'm not a deranged
prophetess bereft of sound judgment, Justice, who
has already sent a sign, will come   475
bearing just triumph in her hands;
she'll come with it,
soon, my child.
The sweet-breathing dream
I just heard   480
reassures me.
For he who has sired you,
the king of the Greeks, is never unmindful

468-71 Chrysothemis' plea to the Chorus to keep silent shows her yet again as fearful and
unheroic after she had mustered the courage to agree to substitute the grave offerings Electra proposed for those that Clytemnestra had given her. At this point we
should imagine Chrysothemis leaving with the libations and with Electra's sash and
lock of hair.

472-515 This is the first choral song (*stasimon*) that the Chorus sing and dance after they
position themselves in the *orchestra*. Electra, who remains onstage, is silent. Encour-
aged by the account of Clytemnestra's dream, which they view as portentous, they
envision a personified Justice, the axe that had been used to murder Agamemnon,
and the Furies all coming together to punish the murderers. The triumphant song
will be followed by news of Orestes' death. March (2001) notes that, in several plays,
Sophocles places a triumphant song just before a catastrophe (*Ajax* 693ff, *Oedipus
the King* 1086ff, *Antigone* 1115ff, *Women of Trachis* 633ff). Here the catastrophe will
not actually materialize, since Orestes is not dead.

of you; nor is the ancient
two-bladed bronze axe   485
that killed him in
a most despicable assault.
She'll come with many feet   *Antistrophe*
and many hands, concealed in fearsome ambushes,   490
the brass-footed Fury.
For an unlawful, unwedded craving for
a blood-defiled marriage came upon
those who have no right to marry.
Because of this, I'm sure   495
beyond doubt that we'll never
ever have a harmless nightmare come
to killers and their accomplices.
Surely there's no prophecy for humankind
in fearful dreams and oracles   500
if this nighttime portent
doesn't reach its due fulfillment.
Oh, Pelops' ancient horsemanship,   *Epode*
cause of so much suffering,   505
how you afflict
this land without end,
ever since Myrtilus was plunged into the sea,
laid prone, hurled
in an execrable outrage   510
headlong from a
golden chariot,

484-87 The axe is conceived of as harboring a grudge against the murderers, who used it in a crime. Jebb (2004): "Such a personification recalls that practice of the Athenian law by which inanimate objects which had caused death were brought into a formal trial."

489-91 Whereas the first stanza of the Choral ode promised the coming of a personified Justice, on the grounds that neither Agamemnon's spirit nor the double-edged axe would allow the crime to be forgotten, the responding stanza envisions the arrival of the Furies, who avenge kindred murder, to carry out the punishment. Furies are also mentioned in lines 112, 276, 1080. On the treatment of the avenging Fury in Sophocles' and Aeschylus' plays, see Winnington-Ingram (1980) 217-239.

504-15 See Introduction 7-8 and 10n. In this epode, the final stanza of their ode, the Chorus name Pelops' conduct as the source of the affliction of Agamemnon's house. In having them do so, Sophocles traces the curse on Agamemnon's house further back by a generation than Aeschylus had done (*Agamemnon* 1583-602, *Libation Bearers* 1068-69). Euripides also traced the curse back to Pelops (*Orestes* 988-96, cf. *Helen* 386-87).

since then never have
afflictions, full of trouble,
left this house.   515

Clytemnestra enters from the palace accompanied by a
maidservant carrying fruit offerings.

Clytemnestra

Free to roam, you're evidently out and about again
now that Aegisthus isn't here — Aegisthus, who always keeps
you indoors, so, being outdoors, you won't shame your kin.
And now with him away, you don't listen to me
at all, but repeatedly rail against me to all and   520
sundry: how presumptuous I am and how unjustly I rule,
and how I treat you and all that's yours abusively.
I'm not abusive, and I speak vilely to you
because you so often speak vilely to me.
For your father, nothing else, is your constant excuse: 525
how he died by my hand. Yes, by my hand,
I know it well. I can't deny it.
But Justice took him, not I alone,
It's Her you'd side with if you had any sense.
For this father of yours, whom you perpetually   530
lament, alone of all the Greeks had the heart
to sacrifice your sister, his own flesh and blood, to the gods — he who,

---

516-822 The second *epeisodion* consists of three scenes. The first (516-659) is an *agôn*, a
debate, between Clytemnestra and Electra on the justice of Agamemnon's murder (see
Essay 105-106), followed by Clytemnestra's prayer to Apollo to avert the harm she
fears, after her portentous dream. In the second (660-803), the Paedagogus enters with
the news of Orestes' death, to which Clytemnestra and Electra react very differently
(see Essay 107-108). In the third (804-822), Electra tells the Chorus of her anguish
and despair. Euripides shows a similar confrontation between mother and daughter
(*Electra* 988-1141), though Aeschylus does not.

516-51 Clytemnestra enters from the center door of the stage-building accompanied by a
maidservant carrying sacrificial gift-offerings for Lycean Apollo (635), whose statue
stands in front of the palace and to whom she will soon pray (634-59).

516-22 Clytemnestra makes much the same point as Chrysothemis had made in 328-29. See
328-29n.

when he sired her, didn't labor with the pain that I endured
when I gave her birth. Fine! Just let me know for whose benefit
he sacrificed her. Would you say it was for the Argives?   535
But they had no right to kill my daughter, having no share in her.
Or was it for his brother, Menelaus? Just tell me —
he killed what was mine and had no intention of paying for it?
Didn't Menelaus have two children of his own?
Wouldn't it have been more fitting for them to die, being the   540
children of the father and mother for whom the voyage
was taken? Or did Hades have some particular
desire for my children — to feast on them, rather than on hers?
Or had your accursed father's love for my children
abated, while his love for Menelaus' children stayed the same?   545
Isn't this the conduct of a thoughtless and wicked father?
I certainly think so, even if you're of a different opinion.
The girl who died would surely say so if she had a voice.
So, for my part, I'm not upset by what was done.
And if you think I'm wrong,   550
you shouldn't find fault with others till you've reached a fair judgment
    yourself.

533-34 In Aeschylus' *Agamemnon* 1417-18, Clytemnestra also refers to the pains of childbirth. The most memorable statement about the pains of labor is that made by Medea: "I would very much rather stand / three times in the front of battle than bear one child" (Euripides, *Medea* 250-51).

534-45 In suggesting a number of possible reasons or motives that Agamemnon could have had for sacrificing his daughter and then promptly negating them, Clytemnestra uses the rhetorical technique called *hypophora*, imagined objection. This was one of the many rhetorical techniques that orators used to make their arguments in the courts and assemblies of the day.

539-42 Sophocles is probably following the account in the pseudo-Hesiodic *Catalogue of Women*, in which Menelaus and Helen have both a son and a daughter (fr. 175 Merkelbach-West). In the *Odyssey* (4. 2-14) Menelaus was said to have a daughter, Hermione, born to Helen, and a son, Megapenthes, born to him of a slave woman once Helen could no longer have children. In the *Iliad* (3.175) Helen mentions having only a daughter.

541 *of the father and mother for whom*: Although the nouns refer to both Menelaus and Helen, the pronoun ('for whom') refers only to Helen. The Argives sailed to Troy to retrieve Menelaus' wife Helen after she had eloped with Paris. By not naming Helen, Clytemnestra conveys her resentment toward the woman who was generally held responsible for causing the Trojan War. That Helen was Clytemnestra's sister is not played up.

549-50 Clytemnestra's total lack of remorse in this play differs from the conduct of her Euripidean namesake, who says that she is not that glad about what she has done (*Electra* 1105-106).

Electra

This time, at least, you can't claim that I said
something hurtful before I heard hurtful things from you.
But if you permit, I'd like to set matters straight
about the dead man and my sister both.   555

Clytemnestra

Of course I permit it! If only you always prefaced your
words like this, it wouldn't be so painful to listen to you.

Electra

Alright, I'll tell you. You say you killed my father.
What statement can be more shameful than this,
whether it was justly done or not? I'll also tell you   560
that you didn't kill him justly, but persuaded
by the wicked man you're living with, who egged you on.
Ask the huntress Artemis the price she exacted
to release the many winds at Aulis.
No, I'll tell you, since we're not allowed to learn from her. 565
My father, as I hear it, once hunting in a grove
sacred to the goddess, startled with his footsteps
a dappled stag with branching horns and, after killing it,

---

561   *persuaded:* The word "persuasion" *(peithô)* in Greek can have erotic connotations. Earlier,
the Chorus had named lust *(erôs)* as Agamemnon's murderer (197). Although Homer had
also recounted that Aegisthus persuaded Clytemnestra to the deed *(Odyssey* 3.264), he
does not give Aegisthus' exact motive. In *Agamemnon*, Aeschylus presents Clytemnestra's
main motive as revenge for the sacrifice of Iphigenia, but also hints at sexual jealousy of
Cassandra, whom Agamemnon had brought back from Troy as a concubine. In *Libation
Bearers* 893-95, however, Aeschylus has her call Aegisthus "beloved" and Orestes state:
"You love this man? Then you shall lie in the same grave with him, and never betray him
even in death." On persuasion, see Buxton (1982) 31-52.

563-74 Artemis was the daughter of Zeus and Leto, Apollo's twin sister. She had the conflict-
ing roles of goddess of hunting and goddess of all uncultivated nature, which made
her the protector of all its young creatures. Sophocles, following the *Cypria* (Davies,
Fragmenta 55-63), makes Agamemnon's offense killing a stag in a grove that was
sacred to her and then boasting of it. Aeschylus *(Agamemnon* 147-50, 191-92) had it
that the Greek fleet could not sail to Troy because Artemis made the winds blow in
the wrong direction. In Sophocles' play, as in the *Cypria*, the problem is that Artemis
stopped the winds from blowing altogether. The detail that the fleet was totally stuck,
and could sail neither to Troy nor back home, is not found in any of the other extant
versions of the story. As van Erp Taalman Kip (1996) 517-521 argues, there is no
reason to believe that the spectators doubted Electra's account because it was new.
Neither Clytemnestra nor anyone else in the play questions it.

564   Aulis, on the coast of Boeotia opposite Euboea, was where the Greeks gathered in
order to sail on their expedition against Troy.

chanced to let slip some boastful remark.
Leto's daughter, angered by this,   570
held back the Achaeans so that my father would
sacrifice his daughter in redress for the animal.
This is how she came to be sacrificed. For there was no other
way out for the army, whether to go home or to Ilion.
This is why, under severe constraint and after much   575
resistance, he sacrificed her, and not for Menelaus' sake.
But even if he had sacrificed her to help
Menelaus — as you claim — did he have to die
for it at your hands? By what law?
Take care that in making such a law for others,   580
you don't make misery and remorse for yourself.
For if we take a life for a life, you, in fact,
would be the first to die, if you got your just deserts.
Be very careful not to put forth a sham plea.
Explain to me, would you, what brings you even now to   585
keep committing the most despicable acts:
sleeping with this man with blood on his hands,
whom you conspired with to murder my father,
and whose children you now bear, while your first, legitimate ones,
born of legitimate wedlock, you cast out.   590
How can I accept all this? Or will you say
that this too is retribution for your daughter?
No! Shame on you if you do! For it's wrong
to marry an enemy because of a daughter.
But it's impossible even to admonish you,   595
because you raise a hue and cry that we revile
our mother. Less a mother than a ruler
to us, that's how I see you, I who lead such a miserable
life, living with so many hardships created
by you and your partner. And your other child,   600
who's abroad, who barely escaped your hand,
poor Orestes, grinds out his unfortunate life.
You've often accused me of raising him

582-83 Electra's warning can be read not only as foreshadowing the murder of Clytemnestra, but also as condemning it. Essay 105-106.

to avenge the blood you spilled. Well, I would have,
you can be sure of it, if I'd been able to. As for   605
all this, trumpet this about me to all the world
if you want. Say that I'm disloyal or sharp tongued, or utterly
without shame. For if by nature I'm accomplished in any of these
things, then I'm surely not putting your nature to shame.

Chorus

I see she's breathing fury. But whether she might have   610
justice on her side, I don't see her giving any thought to this.

Clytemnestra

What thought should I give her
when she's so insolent toward the one who bore her,
and at such an age too?! Do you think
there's something she'll not do out of shame?   615

Electra

Actually, I do feel shame about this,
even if you don't think so. And I realize
that I'm behaving unreasonably and contrary
to my nature. But your enmity
and your actions force me to behave like this against my will.   620
For ugly deeds are taught by ugly deeds.

Clytemnestra

You shameless creature! I and my words
and my actions really make you say too much!

Electra

It's you who says these words, not I. For you
do the deeds, and deeds find their words.   625

Clytemnestra

By the mistress Artemis, you won't escape punishment
for your impudence as soon as Aegisthus returns.

612-13 Judging from her next speech (614-15), Clytemnestra evidently takes their words to
    refer to her. However, coming right after Electra's lengthy and agitated speech (558-
    609), the description of "breathing fury" seems to refer to Electra. In fact, neither
    mother nor daughter considers the justice of the other's point of view. Might there be
    an intentional ambiguity?

626   *by the mistress Artemis*: There is some irony in Clytemnestra's choice of a goddess,
    considering that it comes so soon after Electra has coldly explained that the sacrifice
    of Iphigenia was the recompense that Artemis demanded for her father's offense.

Electra

You see! You're carried away by anger. Even though you said
I could say whatever I want, you don't know how to listen!

Clytemnestra

Won't you let me make my offerings in silence,   630
now that I've allowed you to say everything you want?

Electra

I'll let you. Go ahead. Make your offerings.
And don't blame my lips, for I won't say any more.

*Clytemnestra walks away from Electra toward the statue of
Apollo, turns to the maidservant, who holds the fruit offerings,
and back to Apollo.*

Clytemnestra

Come, my attendant, lift up my offering
of every sort of fruit, so that I may send up a prayer   635
to Lord Apollo to free me from my fears.
Please hear me, Phoebus, our protector,
even though my speech is veiled. For my prayer isn't being
relayed among friends, and it's not advisable to disclose
everything to the light of day with her standing beside me,   640
lest with her malice and garrulous tongue
she spread malicious rumors all over the city.
But listen to me like this, for in this way I too will tell it.
If the ambiguous dream I had last night,
Lycean lord, brings good tidings,   645
grant its fulfillment, but if they're inimical,
make them rebound on my enemies.
And if there are those who'd like to cheat me

---

644   *ambiguous dream*: The ambiguity must stem from the fact that although the dream
      brings Agamemnon back to life, it does not explicitly threaten Clytemnestra.

645   *Lycean lord*: Lycean Apollo is often invoked as a destroyer of enemies. The derivation
      and original meaning of the epithet "Lycean" are uncertain. Clytemnestra calls upon
      Apollo three times (635, 645, 655). Electra too will invoke him in 1376.

648   *those who'd like to cheat me*: The audience was likely to notice Clytemnestra's remark-
      able intuition. Orestes claimed that Apollo instructed him to exact vengeance using
      cunning and guile (36-37). It should be noted that this is also the tactic that Clytem-
      nestra used in murdering Agamemnon. But as much as she feared being deceived, she
      failed to see through the Paedagogus' deception and thought that his news of Orestes'
      death was the fulfillment of her prayer.

of the prosperity I now enjoy, don't let them,
but grant that I forever live my life unharmed   650
and continue to rule the house of Atreus and wield this scepter
in the happy company of the friends whose company I now
enjoy and with those of my children who
harbor no ill will toward me or a bitter grudge.
Please hear my prayer with favor, Lycean Apollo,   655
and grant us all exactly what we ask.
As for the rest, about which I'm silent,
I trust that you, being a god, know it full well,
for, of course, the children of Zeus can see all things.

The Paedagogus enters by one of the side entrances.

Paedagogus
Dear ladies, how can I learn for sure   660
whether this is the house of King Aegisthus?

Chorus
This is it, stranger; your guess is correct.

Paedagogus
And can I also surmise correctly that this lady is his
wife? For in appearance she looks strikingly like a queen.

Chorus
Most certainly! This is her right here.   665

Paedagogus
Greetings to you, My Lady. I come bearing glad
news for you and Aegisthus from a friend.

Clytemnestra
I welcome your words, but first I'd like
you to tell me who sent you.

Paedagogus
Phanoteus of Phocis, to convey a matter of great importance.   670

---

649   *prosperity*: Kells (1973) points out (657f) that: "Orestes too prayed for wealth (72), and
that the Greeks on the whole had a high regard for material prosperity." Aeschylus'
Orestes shows a similar concern to regain the wealth he lost with his father's murder
and Aegisthus' usurpation of the throne (*Libations Bearers* 479-80). In Euripides'
play, however, wealth is associated with the evil of the royal couple and poverty with
the goodness of the farmer to whom Electra has been married.

Clytemnestra

What matter, stranger? Tell me. For I'm sure
you're coming from a friend and will convey a friendly message.

Paedagogus

Orestes is dead – to put it succinctly.

Electra

What a misery! Today is the end of me!

Clytemnestra

What are you saying? What are you saying, stranger? Don't pay any
attention to her!   675

Paedagogus

Orestes is dead. This is what I say now and what I said.

Electra

I'm done for, unfortunate me. Finished.

Clytemnestra

You mind your own business! You, stranger,
tell me the truth: How did he die?

Paedagogus

Since this is what I was sent to do, I'll tell you everything.   680
Having gone to the renowned showpiece
of Greece, the Delphic competitions,

---

679   *How did he die?* The lines may be read either as showing Clytemnestra trying to make
      sure that Orestes is really dead or responding with a mother's interest in knowing
      every detail of how her son died.

680-763 The Paedagogus' story bringing the "news" of Orestes' death belongs to the category
      of messenger speeches in Greek drama. All three tragedians use such speeches to
      provide information from far away places or that could not be staged in the ancient
      theater. This messenger's speech, the longest speech in Sophocles' extant tragedies,
      is considered the most vivid, stirring, and splendid in the playwright's surviving
      work. The detailed description of the chariot race (699-763) is a dramatic reworking
      of the Homeric race in the funeral games in honor of Patroclus (*Iliad* 23.271-611).
      See Barrett (2002) 132-167, Marshall (2006). It's of interest that Orestes chose to
      pretend that he had died in a chariot race, since Sophocles makes Myrtilus' death in
      a chariot race the start of the tragedy that befell the House of Atreus. The inclusion of
      the Pythian Games in this play was criticized in antiquity as an anachronism, since
      they were instituted only in 582 BCE, long after the period in which the play is set
      (see Aristotle, *Poetics* 1460a31-2).

682   *Delphic Games*: also called the Pythian Games, see 49n. The fact that these games
      were held in honor of Apollo is doubly important here: Apollo sent Orestes to avenge
      his father, and Clytemnestra has just prayed to Apollo to protect her from such ven-
      geance.

when he heard the herald's ringing proclamation
announcing the foot-race, which was to be decided first, he entered
the contest, a brilliant figure, a wonder to all who were there.   685
With his running as good as his looks,
he won the race and came out with a glorious prize.
To put it briefly, though there's much to tell,
I've never known a man with such achievements and victories.
One thing you should know: in all the races the umpires
    announced,   690
[...]
he won all the prizes and was
cheered when the herald introduced
him as an Argive named Orestes,
son of Agamemnon, who long ago had assembled   695
the well known army of Greece.
This is how things were. But when a
god rains down disaster, not even a man of might
can escape it. Another day, when a chariot race was held
at sunrise, he entered the race with many others.   700
One charioteer was from Achaea, one from Sparta. There were
two masters of yoked chariots from Libya.
And he, Orestes, with his Thessalian mares,
was the fifth. The sixth charioteer, with chestnut
horses, was from Aetolia, the seventh from   705
Magnesia, the eighth, with white horses, an Aenian.
The ninth was from Athens, built by the gods, and
then, driving the tenth, a Boeotian.
And they stood where the appointed judges
had placed them by lot and stationed their chariots.   710
At the sound of the bronze trumpet they shot out,
shouting all at once at their horses and shaking the reins
in their hands. The entire race-track filled with
the din of rattling chariots, and dust rose up.
And all at once they became a single mass   715
and none spared the goad, as each driver strove to overtake
the axles and neighing horses of the others.

---

691   This line is corrupt in the Greek text and cannot be translated.

The horses' breaths foamed against their
backs and their whirling wheels and kept pushing at them.
Orestes, keeping a hairsbreadth from the pillar,   720
at each round loosened the reins of his
right-hand trace-horse and held back the left horse.
Till that point, all the chariots were still upright. But then,
the Aenian's hard-mouthed colts
bolted and right after turning the post, as they   725
completed the sixth round and had started on the seventh,
collided head-on with the Barcaean chariot.
From this single incident, all the charioteers
smashed and crashed into one another, and the entire plain
of Crisa filled with the wreckage of chariots.   730
But the Athenian, a shrewd driver, seeing what was
happening, pulled his horses to the side and reined
them in, dodging the confusion of horses in the middle of the track.
Orestes was driving last, holding back his
colts, confident of the finish.   735
When he saw that only the Athenian was left,
he sent a sharp cry through the ears of his
swift horses and gave chase. They raced
yoke to yoke, now one driver, then the other,
thrust his head in front of his rival's chariot.   740
Unfortunate Orestes had safely driven all the
other rounds, upright in his upright chariot;

720-23 The most dangerous places in a chariot race were the two turning points, each marked
by a stone post or pillar. The skilled charioteer would try to make the most economical
turn possible by getting as close as he could to the post without touching it, lest he
break his wheel. Orestes was driving a four-horse chariot. The two middle horses were
fastened by harness to the chariot-pole, whereas the outer two horses were secured
by a trace—a strap connecting the horse's harness to the chariot—and controlled by
the reins. This helped the charioteer to manage the chariot on the turn. Orestes was
turning the post from right to left. He thus reined in the near horse, which was on
his left and closest to the post, while giving room to the right trace-horse to make a
larger turn. In other words, he did what had to be done to round the post as close to
it as possible. In the Pythian Games, a charioteer had to execute twelve rounds of
the course (Pindar, *Pyth.* 5.33), which, according to Jebb (2004, 726f.), amounted to
almost five and half miles. Until the accident, Orestes managed to bring his nave as
close as it could be to the post in each of the rounds. Scholars assume that the disaster
happened in the twelfth round.

but then he slackened his left rein as his near horse
was turning the post and, not noticing it, struck the side
of the pillar. He broke the axle-box right down the middle,   745
and was thrown over the chariot rail and entangled
in the sharp-cut reins. When he fell to the ground
his horses bolted wildly into the center of the course.
When the crowd saw he'd fallen from
his chariot, they let out a loud cry for the young man   750
who had done so much only to fall victim to such a misfortune.
One moment tossed to the ground, the next his
legs sticking up toward the sky, until the charioteers
with difficulty brought his bounding horses under control
and untangled him, all covered with blood, so that none of   755
his friends who saw him could recognize the hapless body.
Straightaway his body was burned on a pyre.
Men appointed from Phocis are bringing, in a small bronze
urn, the mere dust of a mighty body,
to draw lots for a grave in his father's land.   760
Such is my story for you, a sad one to tell,
but for those of us who saw it with our own eyes,
the greatest misfortune I've ever seen.

Chorus
Oh! The entire family of our ancient masters,
it seems, is totally destroyed, root and branch.   765

743-45 Instead of tightening the left rein of the left trace-horse and slackening that of the right
   trace-horse, Orestes slackened the left rein. This reduced his control over the horse
   close to the post marker and caused his wheel to strike the stone.
746-47 *entangled in the sharp-cut reins*: Charioteers wound the reins around their bodies
   for greater control.

Clytemnestra
Oh Zeus! What am I to say about this? That it's a piece of good luck?
That it's terrible but welcome? It's a sad thing
to save my life through my own misfortunes.

Paedagogus
Lady, why are you disheartened by what I've told you?

Clytemnestra
It's a wondrous thing to give birth. For even   770
when you're treated badly, you can't hate your own children.

Paedagogus
So I've come in vain, it seems.

Clytemnestra
Certainly not in vain. How can you say "in vain"
if you've come here with sure proofs for me
of the death of him, who having sprung from my life,   775
abandoned my suckling and my nurture and took himself off
and became an exile and a foreigner and never again saw me
after he left this land, but, charging me with his father's murder,
threatened to do dreadful things to me,
so neither by night nor day could sweet sleep   780
shelter me, but from moment to moment
I always lived in fear of death?
But now, today, I'm freed of my fear

766-71 In his comment on 680-763, Kells (1973) points out that the Paedagogus' speech
is more important for its emotional impact on Clytemnestra than on Electra. The
accolades showered on Orestes (685-87, 689-90), whom Clytemnestra has not seen
since he was a child, coupled with the threat he posed to her, must have aroused in
her an odd admixture of emotions: pride in her son's achievements and both sorrow
and relief at his death. Her two utterances here are the sincere outcry of a mother in
a whirlwind of contradictory emotions of love and hate. She knows that she is better
off with him dead than alive, and yet cannot rejoice in it. This complexity of emotions
might be very transient, but the sincerity of this moment should not be overlooked.
Here Clytemnestra does react as a mother would. And this motherly reaction will not
be forgotten by the spectators when she is murdered by the son for whom she grieved,
however briefly. See Essay 107.

of him and of this girl. This girl, who was the greater mischief,
living at my side, draining away my very   785
life's blood. Now we'll spend our days
untroubled by this girl's threats.

Electra

How wretched I am! Now, Orestes, I can
cry over your misfortune when this is your situation and
you're treated with such contempt by our mother. Aren't I well off? 790

Clytemnestra

You're certainly not well off, but he, as he is, is well off.

Electra

Hear her, Nemesis of him who has just died!

Clytemnestra

Nemesis heard what she needed to hear and approved it readily.

Electra

Go on, lord it over me now that you're in luck.

Clytemnestra

Won't you and Orestes stop it already?   795

Electra

We ourselves have been stopped; I can't say how we'll stop you.

784-87 Although Clytemnestra has just described how Orestes' threats had kept her from
 sleeping (778-82), here she says that she no longer fears Electra's threats. Her fear
 of Orestes was well grounded, in that revenge was regarded as a man's task. However, it was Electra's unending rebuke that constantly kept the danger he posed in
 Clytemnestra's mind. The shift highlights the intense mother-daughter conflict that
 runs through the play.

791 Electra succeeds in bringing out the worst in Clytemnestra. Sophocles makes Clytemnestra's words as ironic as possible. Orestes is indeed well off, as the spectators
 know. He is alive and on the brink of avenging his father.

792-93 Nemesis is the personification of the gods' resentment of and punishment for insolence,
 or *hybris*, toward them. Electra appeals to Nemesis as the divinity who should punish
 Clytemnestra for her affront to the dead Orestes. Clytemnestra retorts that Nemesis
 brought death on Orestes as a punishment for his threat to kill his mother. What Nemesis needed to hear were Orestes' threats. What she approved was his death.

795 *Won't you and Orestes stop it already?* It is noteworthy that Clytemnestra includes
 Orestes in her question, even though she believes he is dead. This suggests that he
 remains a living presence in her consciousness.

Clytemnestra

Your coming, stranger, deserves a large reward
if it really stops this girl's garrulous tongue.

Paedagogus

Then I should be on my way, if all is well.

Clytemnestra

Oh no! Since neither you nor our ally who   800
sent you received a proper welcome from me,
please come inside, and leave her outside here to clamor
about her own sorrows and those of her near and dear.

*Clytemnestra, the maidservant, and the Paedagogus go into the
palace. Electra and the Chorus remain outside.*

Electra

Does she look like a grieving and suffering
mother who bitterly weeps and mourns   805
for her unfortunate son, who died in such a manner?
No, she's gone off gloating. Oh, how unhappy I am!
My dearest Orestes, how you've destroyed me with your death!
You've gone and torn from my heart
the only hope I still had left — that you would live   810
and one day come back to avenge our father
and wretched me. But now where should I turn?
For I'm alone, bereft of both you
and our father. Now I must again be
a slave among those I most hate: 815
my father's murderers. Am I well off?
No — I won't live out the rest of my life
with them, but here at this gate
will lay myself down and, friendless, see my life ebb away.
So if someone inside is put out by what I do,   820
let them kill me. For it would be a kindness for
someone to kill me and anguish to live. I have no more desire for life.

818-19 *but here at this gate will lay myself down*: March (2001) envisions Electra collaps-
ing. This would have been difficult given the cumbersome shoes, clothing and mask
worn by Athenian actors; it would also have made it difficult for the actor to project
his voice in the large theater.

Chorus
> Where are the thunderbolts of Zeus,   *Strophe*
> where is the blazing Sun, if looking at these
> things they complacently gloss over them?   825

Electra
> Oh what heartache!

Chorus
> Oh daughter, why are you crying?

Electra
> Oh!

Chorus
> Don't shriek so extravagantly.

Electra
>   You're killing me.

Chorus
>   How?   830

Electra
> If you hold out hope
> for those who've clearly gone
> to Hades, you trample even more   835
> on me as I waste away.

823-70 In this short duet, the Chorus try to rouse Electra from her despair following the news
of Orestes' supposed death by comparing her situation to that of mythical examples
and showing her that other people have also suffered great misfortunes.

832-35 It is not clear whether the hope is on behalf of those who have gone to Hades (e.g., that
Orestes and Agamemnon will have the gratification of seeing Agamemnon's murder
avenged) or that those in Hades will help Electra accomplish the vengeance. The
latter reading would be consistent with the ancient Greek belief that the dead could
act in the world of the living (459-60, 967-69, 986-87; Aeschylus, *Libation Bearers*
476-509), but either reading seems possible.

Chorus   *Antistrophe*
   But I know that Lord Amphiaraus,
   who was swallowed up by the earth through a woman's golden
   snares, now underground...
Electra
   Oh what heartache!   840
Chorus
   ...rules with his spirit full of power.
Electra
   Oh!
Chorus
   Yes, indeed! For she, his murderess,...
Electra
                              was killed.
Chorus
                                        Yes.   845

Electra
   I know. I know! An avenger
   appeared for him in his sorrow;
   but I have no one any more, for the one
   I had is gone, snatched away.
Chorus   *Strophe*
   Unhappy you, unhappiness is your lot!
Electra
   I know this well, all too well,   850
   I, whose life, through all the months that
   flow one into the other, is one of many terrible afflictions.

---

838   *Amphiaraus* was one of the seven heroes who fought in the ill-fated expedition against
        Thebes, aimed at securing the rule of the city for Polyneices. At first, he refused to
        join, since, being a seer, he knew he would die in the fighting; but he was persuaded to
        go by his wife, Eriphyle, whom Polyneices had bribed with a golden necklace. Before
        leaving for the war, he commanded his children to avenge his death by killing their
        mother and by making a second expedition against the city. As he attacked Thebes,
        he was driven off. The gods, however, thought he was too good a man to be killed
        there, so had him swallowed up by the earth instead.

846   *an avenger*: Electra refers to Alcmaeon, Amphiaraus' son, who killed his mother,
        Eriphyle, for her treachery (838n) and, like Orestes, was driven into exile.

Chorus

We know what you mean.

Electra

Then don't lead me on

any more when there's no —   855

Chorus

What are you saying?

Electra

when there's no longer the comfort

of hope from a brother born of the same noble father.

Chorus   *Antistrophe*

Death is the fate of all mortals.   860

Electra

Is it also fate to die in swift races the way

that he, unfortunate that he is, died,

entangled in raw-cut reins?

Chorus

His mangled body is unimaginable.

Electra

How could it not be, since in a foreign land   865

untended by my hands...

Chorus

Alas!

Electra

...he's buried, without a funeral

and without a funeral song from me.   870

*Chrysothemis enters through one of the side entrances, catching
her breath.*

Chrysothemis

I'm so excited, my dearest sister,

I've put aside all decorum to rush here as quickly as possible.

I bring you joy and relief from the

miseries you had and complained about.

865-70 Tending to the corpse was the proper rite and customary prerogative of close female
relatives.

Electra

And where could you find an antidote for my   875
sufferings, for which there is no longer a cure?

Chrysothemis

Orestes is here with us – mind you hear what
I'm saying. It's as plain as you see me!

Electra

Have you gone stark out of your mind, poor girl?
Are you mocking both your suffering and mine?   880

Chrysothemis

No, by our father's hearth, I'm not
mocking you: he really is here with us.

Electra

You poor girl, where on earth
have you heard this story that you so completely believe it?

Chrysothemis

I believe the clear signs I've seen with   885
my own eyes, not anyone's story.

Electra

You poor girl, what proof have you seen? What did
you see that you're enflamed by such an incurable fire?

Chrysothemis

For god's sake! Listen, so that after learning the rest
you can decide whether I'm in my right mind or addled.   890

Electra

Very well, then, tell me, if you get pleasure from the story.

Chrysothemis

Very well, I'll tell you everything I saw.
When I went to our father's ancestral grave,
I saw streams of milk freshly flowing from

893-915 Chrysothemis' interest is piqued when she sees the libations of milk and flowers
at her father's grave, but it is her identification of the lock of hair at the gravesite as
Orestes' that leads her to deduce that Orestes is back in Argos. The lock of hair plays
a role in Aeschylus' and Euripides' recognition scenes as well (Aeschylus, *Libation
Bearers* 167-80; Euripides, *Electra* 513-33). Chrysothemis' description of her visit
to Agamemnon's grave bears many similarities to the Old Man's visit to his grave in
Euripides' *Electra* 509-19.

the top of the mound and our father's grave   895
decked all around with every sort of flower.
I was amazed by the sight and looked around
to see whether anyone was coming my way.
When I saw that the entire place was still,
I approached the grave, and there I saw,   900
near the top of the mound, a lock of newly cut hair.
As soon as I saw it, unhappy me,
I was struck by a familiar image, telling me it's
a token of Orestes, dearest to me of all mortals.
I took it in my hands, not saying a word of ill-omen,   905
but instantly, in my joy, my eyes filled with tears.
And I fully know now, as I knew then, that this
pleasing gift came from none other than him.
Who else but you or I would do this?
And I didn't, that much I know, and neither did you.   910
For how could you? You're not allowed to step out of
the house even to make offerings to the gods without being punished.
And it's not the sort of thing our mother
does—and it wouldn't escape notice if she had.
These are grave offerings from Orestes.   915
Cheer up, my dear. The same fortune doesn't

895-901 The Greek word can be translated *grave*, *sepulcher*, or *tomb*. It is difficult to know
which one to select because there was no single way of burying the dead in Homer's
or Sophocles' times. The method varied from town to town, village to village. Sometimes the cremated remains, placed in an urn, would be buried in a large hole dug in
the ground, which would be filled and topped with another urn, this one empty, that
served as a marker. This empty urn would sometimes be stood on a mound that had
been constructed over the grave and covered other urns and burnt remains. Sometimes
a mound of earth was raised above the burial place. It is on top of such a mound that
Chrysothemis saw the lock. See, Kurtz and Boardman (1971) 68-108; Sourvinou-
Inwood (1995) 108-147; Garland (2001) 34-37.

903-904 In having Chrysothemis recognize Orestes' lock of hair, Sophocles moved up a key
element of the recognition scene in Aeschylus' play, in preparation for making the
recognition in his own play (1174-225) more natural and less contrived. In Aeschylus'
play, Electra recognizes her brother through his footprints and the lock of hair he left at
his father's grave (*Libation Bearers* 165-211). Euripides pokes fun at the implausibility
of this recognition, having his Electra say that a man's and woman's feet are not the
same, the ground is too hard to see prints, etc. (*Electra* 524-46).

905   Chrysothemis said no word of ill omen so not to spoil the happy moment. This probably means that she said nothing, as the Greek "to say a good omen" means to keep
silent. There is actually little she could have said that wouldn't have risked revealing
Orestes' presence.

always come to the same people.
Things were terrible for us in the past; maybe today will mark
the start of better things for us in the future.

Electra

How I pity you for your naiveté.   920

Chrysothemis

What's the matter? Doesn't what I'm saying make you happy?

Electra

You have no clue where you are in this world or what you're thinking.

Chrysothemis

How can I not know what I saw clearly?

Electra

You poor girl, he's dead! And any chance of rescue
for you is gone with him. Look no more to him!   925

Chrysothemis

You poor girl! Who did you hear this from?

Electra

From someone who was there when he died.

Chrysothemis

Where is this man? I'm really astounded.

Electra

In the house. Agreeable to our mother and not at all displeasing to her.

Chrysothemis

Oh unhappy me! So whose were   930
these lavish offerings at our father's grave?

Electra

If you ask me, I think that someone placed
them in memory of the dead Orestes.

Chrysothemis

How wretched I am! And I rushed with such
joy with my news, not knowing the   935
disaster we were really in. And now that I'm
here, I find new miseries on top of the old ones.

Electra

This is how things are. But if you listen to me,
you'll lighten the weight of our present misery.

Chrysothemis

What? Will I bring the dead to life some day?   940

Electra

No, that's not what I meant. I'm not such a fool.

Chrysothemis

Then what are you telling me to do that's in my power to do?

Electra

To have the courage to do what I advise.

Chrysothemis

If it will do any good, I won't refuse.

Electra

Nothing succeeds without effort.   945

Chrysothemis

Alright, I'll help as much as I can.

Electra

Then listen to how I've decided to bring the matter to conclusion.
Regarding help from our loved ones, you're well aware
that we don't have anyone. Hades took them
from us, and we two are left alone.   950
I, as long as I was hearing that our brother lived
and prospered, I had hopes he'd come
one day to be the avenger of our father's murder.
But now that he's gone, I count on you
not to shrink from killing, along with me, your sister, the man   955
who by his own hand murdered our father:

938-89 Rising out of her desperation that Orestes' death has put an end to any possibility
of revenge, Electra comes up with the idea that she and her sister will do the job
themselves.

Aegisthus. I mustn't keep secrets from you anymore.
For to what end will you remain idle? On what hope
that's still there will you fix your gaze? You must regret
being robbed of our father's great wealth.   960
You must feel pain that at this point of your life
you're growing old, unmarried and unwedded.
Well, don't harbor any hopes that you'll ever
be. Aegisthus isn't a stupid man.
He'll never allow you or me to have   965
children, who'd clearly be a scourge to him.
But if you listen to what I advise, first of all,
you'll win praise for piety from our dead
father below and from our brother too.
Second, people will call you a free woman,   970
which is what you were born, and you'll find a marriage worthy
of you. For people generally cast their sights on quality.
Don't you see the great fame you'll surely win
for yourself and me by doing what I say?
For who, whether a citizen or a foreigner,   975
looking at us won't greet us with praise:
"Look, my friends, at these two sisters,
who saved their father's house, who without
regard for their own lives came forth as avengers
of murder against foes sitting strong and secure.   980
We should all love them, we should all revere them;

---

957   *Aegisthus*: The play suggests that Electra's naming Aegisthus as the sole target of
their revenge was an intentional ploy to induce Chrysothemis to join in the scheme.
From previous statements, it is clear that Electra viewed her mother as a full partner
in Agamemnon's murder (97-99, 205-206, 585-88) and, moreover, that she hadn't
temporarily forgotten about her, since she had mentioned Clytemnestra only a few
moments earlier, in the gratuitous statement that the news of Orestes' death was not
displeasing to her (929). Her sole focus on Aegisthus, the male enemy, better enables
Electra to draw the revenge as a heroic act on the part of brave women, while avoiding
confronting her sister with the horror of killing her own mother.

973-85 Electra's argument that Aegisthus will never allow her or her sister to marry and bear
children is sound enough, and we may also accept that their dead father and brother
might commend their piety and loyalty after they take revenge. But when she moves
to the presumed reaction of the society to their vengeance, Electra is on very shaky
grounds. Fame for heroic acts was mainly a masculine value in ancient Greece. How
much would the citizens of Argos really have admired the two sisters for acting like
men? And even if valiant women were admired, we may wonder whether they would
have been viewed as desirable wives.

and at festivals and all the gatherings of the city,
we should all honor them for their bravery."
Such things, I tell you, everyone will proclaim of us,
whether we're alive or dead, so our fame will never cease.   985
My dear sister, listen to me, work with our father,
work with our brother, free me from evil,
and free yourself too. You know very well that
living dishonorably is shameful to those who are noble by nature.

Chorus
In matters like this, prudent forethought is an ally   990
both to the one who speaks and to the one who listens.

Chrysothemis
Yes. And before she spoke, ladies, if she had
good sense she would have
remembered caution, but she doesn't remember.
What have you set your sights on that you've armed   995
yourself with such boldness and demand that I help you?
Don't you see? You were born a woman, not a man;
physically, you're not as strong as your enemies.
Their fortune flourishes day by day,
while ours dwindles to nothing.   1000
Who, then, who plots to kill such a man
can escape unscathed by disaster?
Be careful that, in our feeble circumstances, we don't
heap more trouble on ourselves if someone hears these words.
No remedy or benefit of any sort will come   1005
if we gain a fine reputation but die dishonorably.
For the worst thing isn't to die, but when one wants
to die, not being able to die.

---

987   In Electra's view, Agamemnon and Orestes are laboring from the Netherworld to
        effect the revenge.

990-91 The Chorus politely advise Electra not to pursue her course, while cautioning Chryso-
        themis not to listen to her.

1006-8 Chrysothemis is less optimistic than Electra about the chances of any attempt at
        revenge on their part succeeding. Her concern is that if they are caught, as she expects,
        they will be slowly tortured to death. This, in her view, will make their death dis-
        honorable. Indicative of her anxiety is that she repeats the verb "to die" three times
        in these lines.

No, I implore you, before we're totally destroyed
and leave our family completely desolate,   1010
rein in your anger. As for what was said, I, for my part,
for your sake, will keep it secret and unacted on.
And you, at long last, would you have the good sense
to yield to power when you have none yourself!

Chorus

Do as she says! There is no greater advantage   1015
than foresight and a sensible mind.

Electra

You're saying nothing I didn't expect. I knew
very well you'd reject my proposal.
Well, I'll just have to do the deed with my own hands,
on my own, because I won't leave it undone.   1020

Chrysothemis

If only you were thus determined when
our father was killed, for then you would have accomplished every-
    thing.

Electra

By nature I was, but my understanding was weaker.

Chrysothemis

Then try to keep this sort of understanding for the rest of your life.

Electra

You're telling me this because you won't help me.   1025

Chrysothemis

Yes, because if I venture it, I'm likely to fare badly.

Electra

I admire your mind, but detest your cowardice.

Chrysothemis

I'll bear it patiently when I hear you praise me too.

Electra

Never! You'll never suffer praise from me.

1028   Chrysothemis is saying that she is as indifferent to Electra's censure now as she will
        be to the praise she will receive from Electra when Electra realizes that her advice
        has been good.

Chrysothemis

Time will tell. We've a long future ahead of us.   1030

Electra

Go away! You're of no help!

Chrysothemis

Oh yes, I am of help, but you're not able to learn!

Electra

Go and tell it all to your mother!

Chrysothemis

Certainly not. I don't hate you enough.

Electra

So understand what dishonor you're leading me to.   1035

Chrysothemis

Not dishonor, but forethought for you.

Electra

So do I have to do what you think is right?

Chrysothemis

Yes. When you're thinking sensibly, you'll lead us both.

Electra

It's really terrible when a person who speaks so well is so off the
    mark!

Chrysothemis

You've described your own failing to a tee.   1040

Electra

How's that? Don't you think that what I'm saying is right?

Chrysothemis

But there are times when even being right brings harm.

Electra

I don't want to live by such laws.

1035   As Electra sees it, she will bring dishonor upon herself if, following Chrysothemis'
    advice, she fails to avenge her father's murder.

1042   Chrysothemis admits implicitly that Electra is right, as she has already conceded in
    337-40, but recommends the more pragmatic and expedient way of conduct.

Chrysothemis
But if you go ahead with what you intend, you'll praise me.

Electra
I'll certainly go ahead with it; I'm not alarmed by you.   1045

Chrysothemis
Will you really? You won't reconsider?

Electra
There's nothing worse than bad advice.

Chrysothemis
Apparently you don't take account of anything I say.

Electra
I made up my mind long ago, not just now.

Chrysothemis
I'll go then. For you can't bring yourself   1050
to accept my words, nor I your ways.

Electra
Go inside then. I'll never ask you for help again,
no matter how much you'd like me to, since
there's no sense in chasing after nothing.

Chrysothemis
Well, if you think you're so smart,   1055
go on being smart, for when you soon
get into trouble, you'll come round to what I'm saying.

Chrysothemis goes into the palace.

1044   Chrysothemis assumes that Electra will come to appreciate the value of her warnings
       when the plot fails.

1049   This is an odd claim, as it's only since Electra "learned" that Orestes was dead that
       she concluded that she would have to carry out the revenge on her own. Up until then,
       she had repeatedly said that she was waiting for Orestes to come and do it and that
       her hopes for revenge were dashed by Orestes' death.

Chorus   *Strophe*
Why, when we see the most prescient
birds on high solicitous of those
from whom they sprang   1060
and from whom they
benefited, do we not repay our parents in the same way?
No, by Zeus' lightning-bolt
and by the heavenly Themis,
trouble won't be long in coming.   1065
Oh news that dwells among
mortals on earth, send down to Atreus' sons
underground a sad message
of dishonor that will bring them no joy.
Tell them that their house is sick,   *Antistrophe* 1070
and that a double battle cry
has gone up between the
two children, and is no longer
tempered by loving ways. Electra, betrayed,
tosses alone in waves of distress,   1075
miserable, forever lamenting the past,

1058-1097 Chrysothemis has entered the royal home, but Electra remains at her place near the
portal, as the Chorus sing and dance in the *orchestra*. The strong support the Chorus
express for Electra here is very different from the caution they had recommended
earlier, both in lines 990-91 and in their first encounter with Electra.

1058-1069 The birds are usually assumed to be storks, which were known for feeding their
parents. The Chorus criticize Chrysothemis for not returning in kind the nurture she
received from Agamemnon. Kells (1973, 1066) argues that the Greek word translated
"benefited" usually refers to the benefit parents derive from their children and, hence,
that the Chorus are mounting a general criticism of the lack of reciprocal affection
and obligations between the generations, in both directions.

1058   *prescient*: alternatively translated "prudent" or "sensible," implies that the birds who
are solicitous of the parents who had nurtured them are not entirely altruistic, but
expect some kind of benefit or reward for their behavior.

1064   *Themis*: Primordial goddess whose name means "law" or "custom," and who was
viewed as the embodiment of divine law, order, and custom.

1066-69 This prayer or request aims to get Agamemnon and Orestes to hurry up and help out
with the revenge before the discord between the sisters brings shame on their house.

1074   *betrayed*: The Chorus do not say who betrayed Electra: whether Chrysothemis, who
refused to join her in her mission of revenge; Agamemnon, who hasn't done enough
to see to it that his death would be avenged; Orestes, who took so long in coming; or
some unnamed god or gods. Their leaving the betrayer unnamed suggests that his or
her identity is not very important, and enables the Chorus to highlight the emotion
that Electra feels as she is left alone in her grief.

like the ever plaintive nightingale.
She's careless of death
and ready to give up the light,
if only she can kill the double Fury.   1080
Who could be born so loyal to a father?
No one who is noble wants to tarnish   *Strophe*
their good name by living a base
and inglorious life. Oh child! Oh child!
This is why you have chosen the   1085
common lot of tears,
overcoming dishonor
so as to win a double renown at one and the same time:
to be called both a wise daughter and the best daughter.
May you surpass your enemies   *Antistrophe* 1090
in power and wealth by as much as
you now live below them;
for I find you
living a most unhappy fate
and yet winning first prize,   1095
through your piety toward Zeus,
for obeying nature's highest laws.

*Orestes, Pylades, and at least two attendants enter through one
of the side entrances. One attendant carries a small bronze urn.
All the party are disguised as Phocians.*

Orestes

Ladies, have we been given the right directions
and come to our destination?

1079   Seeing the light is a common metaphor in Greek literature for being alive, not seeing
       it for being dead.

1081   The line can also be translated "Who could have such a noble father?" This transla-
       tion would suggest that the Chorus view Electra's readiness to die for her father as
       her living up to the expectations of her noble birth.

1097   *nature's highest laws*: These are the unwritten laws of the gods, as opposed to the
       laws which humans decide for their own particular needs. Cf. Sophocles, *Antigone*
       454-55.

1098-175 The action returns. Orestes and Pylades enter through one of the wings accompa-
       nied by some attendants. One of the attendants must be carrying the bronze urn that
       supposedly contains Orestes' ashes. The audience, having seen them at the start of
       the play, know who they are, but the Chorus do not.

Chorus

What are you asking? What is it you want?   1100

Orestes

All the way here I've been inquiring where Aegisthus lives.

Chorus

You've reached your destination. Your guides can't be faulted.

Orestes

Which of you
will tell the people in the house
of our long-awaited arrival?

Chorus

This lady, if the closest relative is the one who should announce it. 1105

Orestes

Go in, lady, and tell those inside that some
men from Phocis are looking for Aegisthus.

Electra,

Oh god! You can't be bringing
solid proof of the report we heard?

Orestes

I don't know of any report. But old   1110
Strophius sent me with news of Orestes.

Electra

What is it, stranger? How fear steals over me!

Orestes

Orestes is dead, and we're bringing his scanty remains
in this small urn you see us carrying.

Electra

Unhappy me! It's clear now.   1115
I see, it seems, a load of grief that can be easily carried.

Orestes

If you're crying over Orestes' misfortune,
know that this vessel houses his body.

1105   *closest relative*: This is the first clue Orestes gets of Electra's identity, but he doesn't
        pick it up at this point.

Electra

Oh stranger, give it to me, I implore you! If he's
concealed in this vessel, give it into my hands to hold,   1120
so that, with these ashes, I may weep
for myself and my entire line.

Orestes turns to one of the attendants.

Orestes

Bring it and give it to her, whoever she is.
For she asks for it not out of enmity, but
as one of his friends or one of his blood.   1125

Electra takes the urn and addresses it, cradling it in her arms.

Electra

O last memento of Orestes' life,
the dearest of men to me. How far from the hopes
with which I sent you forth, I take you now into my arms.
Now all that I hold in my hands is nothingness,
even though, my child, I sent you forth from home resplendent.   1130
How I wish I'd died before that moment,
before I sent you to a foreign land, stealing you away
with these two hands and saving you from murder,
so that on that day you would have been killed,
and received your portion of our father's grave.   1135
As it is, far from home, an exile in a foreign land,
you died miserably, far from your sister.
I didn't, I'm sad to say, wash you and deck

1126-70 Up till now we have seen that Electra is imbued with deep hatred for her mother and
Aegisthus. This speech, full of pathos and tenderness, shows that Electra can love
too. Aulus Gellius, the second century CE author of *Attic Nights* (6.5), tells us that the
fourth-century BCE actor Polus recited this speech while mourning the death of his
recently deceased son. Although the formal recognition has not yet taken place, Orestes
might guess who Electra is from this speech. The mutual recognition of the principal
characters is treated differently by the three tragedians. See Essay 108-111.

1130   *child, I sent you forth from home resplendent*: Electra treats Orestes as if he were
her own child. She is as proud of him as any mother, and grieves his loss as a mother
would.

your corpse with hands that loved you, nor raise up this
sad burden out of the blazing fire, as would have been fitting.   1140
No, you were tended by strangers' hands, poor you,
and arrived here as a small weight in a small urn.
My long ago nurture of you
has come to nothing, the nurture I always gave
you with such sweet toil. You were never   1145
more loved by your mother than by me.
I was your nurse, no one else in the house;
I was the one you always called "sister."
And now, all this has vanished in a day
with your death. Like a whirlwind, you   1150
swept everything away and are gone. Our father is gone,
and with you I've also died; for you are dead and gone,
and our enemies are laughing. Our mother, who is no mother,
is delirious with joy – the mother you often
sent me secret messages telling you would come   1155
in person to punish. But this evil daimon,
yours and mine, has snatched this away and
sent you to me as ashes and an empty shadow
instead of the form I loved.
Oh my!   1160
Oh!
Alas! Alas!
You who were sent on a dreadful journey, my dearest, how you've
destroyed me! Yes, destroyed me! Oh, my dear brother,
admit me into this little urn of yours,   1165
nothing to nothing, so that with you I may dwell
below forever. For when you were on earth,

1139-40 When the body was cremated and not inhumed, the mourners collected the ashes
    after the body was burned and placed them in a funerary urn (*Iliad,* 23.237-44,
    250-54; 24.791-98*).* The urn would be placed in a grave and a mound raised over the
    grave. See also 895-901n.

1148   *I was the one:* The Greek does not have exactly this phrase, but uses the personal
    pronoun "I" where the grammar does not require it. This "I" highlights Electra's
    singularity vis á vis her sisters. It implies that Electra was the only one of Orestes'
    sisters that he actually called "sister." Jebb (2004) reads the statement as suggesting
    that Electra represented for Orestes "all that 'sister' means." Alternatively, we may
    read the statement as reflecting Electra's own elevated view of her place in Orestes'
    life.

I shared everything with you equally, and now in my
death I ask not to be denied my share of your grave.
For the dead, I see, no longer suffer pain.   1170

Chorus
Remember, Electra, you were born to a mortal father
and Orestes was mortal. So don't grieve so much.
This is a debt that all of us must pay.

Orestes
What shall I say? Where can I possibly find words?
I'm at a loss for words! I can no longer command my tongue.   1175

Electra
What's suddenly upset you? What do you mean?

Orestes
Do I see the illustrious image of Electra?

Electra
Yes, wretched as she is.

Orestes
What a terrible misfortune!

Electra
Surely, stranger, you're not upset about me?   1180

Orestes
Oh body so disgracefully and godlessly wasted!

Electra
There's no one else here, stranger, that your woeful words describe.

Orestes
How sad your unwedded, wretched state!

Electra
Why are you looking at me so intently, stranger, and sighing so?

1174-75 Following Electra's identification of herself as Orestes' sister in line 1148 and the
Chorus' addressing her by name in 1171, Orestes finally realizes who she is.

1174-231 Revealing that he recognizes her, Orestes carefully leads Electra to recognize him as
the brother she has been mourning. The dialogue, consisting of single line exchanges
(*stichomythia*) and division of the line between two characters (*antilabê*), amplifies
the tension inherent in the situation.

1177   *illustrious image of Electra*: Electra is illustrious, famous, because she is the daughter
of a famous man.

Orestes

How little I knew of my own sorrows!   1185

Electra

What was said that made you realize this?

Orestes

Seeing all your tribulations.

Electra

You really see very few of my afflictions.

Orestes

Is there anything worse than this to see?

Electra

That I live with the murderers.   1190

Orestes

With whose murderers? Where does this abomination you insinuate
come from?

Electra

My father's. Their slave I am against my will.

Orestes

But who on earth subjects you to such constraint?

Electra

A mother she's called, but resembles a mother in nothing.

Orestes

How? By hitting you or by daily abuse?   1195

Electra

By hitting me and abusing me and every kind of mistreatment.

Orestes

And is there anyone to help you or to stop her?

1191   Although Orestes knows that his sister stands before him, he still does not reveal his
        identity, but asks questions whose answers he probably knows. His questions serve to
        convey his care for Electra and to enable the audience to hear yet again of the abuse
        that Electra suffers in her father's home.

1192   "My father's," answers Orestes' first question (1191), which asks with whose murder-
        ers Electra lives. It is somewhat jarring, because we expect an answer to his second
        question in line 1191, which asks the source of the abomination. The *non-sequitur*
        highlights Electra's obsession with her father.

Electra

No one at all. For you've shown me the ashes of the one I had.

Orestes

Oh ill-starred girl! How I pity you when I look at you!

Electra

Then know that you're the only one alive who's ever pitied me.   1200

Orestes

Yes, I'm the only one who's come feeling pain for your afflictions.

Electra

Surely you're not a kinsman from somewhere!

Orestes

I'll tell you, [*pointing at the Chorus*] if these ladies here can be
trusted.

Electra

They can be trusted, so you can speak in confidence.

Orestes

Then put this urn aside, so you can learn everything.   1205

Electra

Please, by the gods, don't do this to me, stranger!

Orestes

Do as I tell you and you won't go wrong!

Electra

By your beard, don't take away what's most precious to me!

Orestes

I'm telling you, I won't let you keep it!

Electra

Oh how wretched I am, Orestes, if I'm deprived of giving you
burial.   1210

1205-220 The struggle over the urn is important. It is by forcing Electra to physically give
up the urn that Orestes makes her realize that he is alive.

1208   *By your beard*: refers to a ritualistic act of supplication, often accompanied by the
touching of the chin and the knees.

Orestes

Say no words of ill-omen. It's not right for you to mourn.

Electra

How can it be not be right for me to mourn my dead brother?

Orestes

It's inappropriate for you to speak of him like this.

Electra

Am I so unworthy of the dead?

[Orestes reaches for the urn and Electra hugs it closer, in a kind of tug of war]

Orestes

You're unworthy of no one. But this urn isn't for you.   1215

Electra

It is, if it's Orestes' body that I hold.

Orestes

But it's not Orestes', except for the contrivance of a tale.

Electra

Where is the poor boy's grave then?

Orestes

There isn't any. A living person doesn't have a grave.

Electra

What are you saying, child?

Orestes

My words carry no deception.   1220

Electra

Then he's alive?

Orestes

If there's life in me!

1211   *words of ill-omen*: Electra's speaking of the living Orestes as dead carried the danger of a statement that could fulfill itself. Orestes is uneasy about this, even though he glibly discounted the idea in 59-60.

Electra

Then you're he?

Orestes

Examine this ring of mine,
which was our father's, and assure yourself whether or not I'm telling
the truth.

Electra

Most joyous day!

Orestes

Most joyous, I agree.

Electra

Oh voice, you've come?

Orestes

Ask no further.   1225

Electra

[*embracing Orestes, who returns her embrace*]
Am I holding you in my arms?

Orestes

So may you hold me always!

Electra [*to the Chorus*]

Oh dearest ladies! Oh fellow townswomen!
Look at Orestes here, dead by a contrivance
and now by a contrivance safely home.

Chorus

We see him, child, and because of this happy   1230
turn of events a tear of joy trickles down from our eyes.

1223-24 The signet ring is the physical token that seals the recognition, but Electra's recognition of Orestes has developed naturally from their conversation. For the significance of the signet ring, see Batchelder (1995) 117-123.

Electra   *Strophe*
Oh child! Child
of the one I loved most,
you came this moment.
You found out, you came, you saw those you longed for.   1235

Orestes
I'm here, but hush and wait!

Electra
What's the matter?

Orestes
It's best to be quiet, so no one inside will hear.

Electra
By Artemis,
ever-virgin, I'll never think it worthy to tremble   1240
because of these useless, burdensome women
who are always in the house.

1232-87 This is the only recognition scene in Sophocles' extant plays that is structured as a
quasi-duet. As soon as Electra realizes that the urn she is holding does not contain
Orestes' ashes, she bursts into song, overjoyed at seeing her brother and forgetting
that her longed-for revenge is still to be carried out. Orestes, ever pragmatic and
mindful of his mission, repeatedly tries to temper her premature joy. Electra's song
consists of a strophe, antistrophe, and epode. Between stanzas, Orestes, not singing,
but speaking in iambic trimeter, tries to calm her down. The variety of lyric meters in
which Electra sings suggests her joy and exhilaration when she realizes that Orestes
is alive and at her side. For a more detailed discussion of this scene, see Roisman
(2000) 190-199. See Essay 110.

1235   *you found out, you came, you saw those you longed for:* This is one of the only two
spoken lines Electra has (the other is 1256) in her song. The statement is arranged
in a highly effective rhetorical figure called a *tricolon*, the best known example of
which is Caesar's *veni, vidi, vici.* The *tricolon's* characteristic asyndeton (omission
of conjunctions that ordinarily join the words or clauses) gives the figure expressive
compactness and decisiveness. The sequence, with "you found out" at the beginning,
supports the idea, suggested in 167-68, that Orestes was aware of Electra's plight before
he arrived. If he was not aware, however, as is suggested by his inquiry into Electra's
situation (1181-202), then the sequence would properly begin with his arrival and the
tricolon would be semantically anacoluthic, or illogical.

        those: The Greek sometimes uses the plural when the reference is singular. The effect
        is to generalize whatever statement is being made.

1239   *Artemis:* Electra's swearing by Artemis conveys her affinity for the goddess who, like
        herself, is a virgin, and also reminds the viewer of her earlier defense of Agamemnon's
        sacrifice of Iphigenia as the necessary recompense for his affront to this goddess
        (563-72).

Orestes

But remember there's Ares
in women too! You know this fully from your own experience, I think.

Electra

Ah!!   1245
You've brought to mind
our sorrows, which by their nature
can never be veiled,
never dispelled, and never forgotten.   1250

Orestes

I know this well. But only when the situation calls for it
should we recall these things.

Electra   *Antistrophe*

Every minute,
every minute at any time is fitting
and right for me to tell these things,   1255
now that my mouth has been freed.

Orestes

I fully agree! So safeguard your freedom.

Electra

By doing what?

Orestes

By not wanting to talk at length when the time isn't right.

Electra

Who could thus   1260
exchange speech for a silence worthy of your appearance,

1243 *Ares*: Ares is the god of war. Here he serves as emblematic of a feisty, combative
     spirit.

1245-50 By reminding Electra that she is a woman who has shown a feisty, combative spirit,
     Orestes suggests that the women in the house can be dangerous, and she should not
     make so much noise. Electra in her excitement does not get his point, but rather
     plunges into self-pity.

1256 *now that my mouth has been freed*: For Electra, Orestes' arrival signifies her freedom,
     even though the revenge has not yet taken place. As her song progresses, she responds
     to single words of Orestes without grasping the danger he tries to convey to her.

1260-63 By asking "who could ...," Electra here generalizes her feelings at finally seeing
     Orestes, then immediately switches to the first person. See 1235n.

now that I've seen you beyond
all expectation and against all hope?

Orestes

You saw me when the gods stirred me to come ...

Electra

You tell me of an even greater   1265
gift than the one you told before; if a god
has brought you to our house.
I consider it a divine act.   1270

Orestes

I'm loath to curb your jubilation, but I fear
you're overcome by too much joy.

Electra   *epode*

You, who after
such a long time finally deemed it right
to come to me in this dearest of journeys,
please don't, having seen me thus full of suffering ...   1275

Orestes

What shouldn't I do?

Electra

                     Don't deprive me
of, don't make me lose, the pleasure of your face.

Orestes

I'd certainly be angry if I saw someone doing this.

Electra

You agree?

Orestes

                     Of course.   1280

Electra

My dear one, I heard a voice
I couldn't hope to hear. I reined in my excitement
and made no sound, and without crying out,
unhappy as I am, I listened to your voice.
And now I have you. You've come   1285
with your dear face, which I
could not forget even in my suffering.

Orestes

Spare me the verbiage. Don't tell me
how wicked our mother is or how Aegisthus
is draining the wealth of our father's   1290
house, squandering and throwing it about.
For words may thwart the opportunity time gives us.
Tell me only what I need to know now,
at the present time: where we should show or hide ourselves so that
on this journey of ours we may put a stop to our enemies' gloating. 1295
And make sure that our mother can't tell
from your radiant face that we two have come against the house.
But sigh, as if over my destruction, though
falsely reported. For when we pull it off, then
we'll be able to rejoice and laugh freely.   1300

Electra

Well, my brother! Whatever suits you
will suit me too, because it's
from you I've taken all my joy, not from
myself. I wouldn't agree to receive a large benefit
for myself at the price of vexing you even a tiny bit, for I   1305
wouldn't be serving properly the god who is with us now.
But you know how things are here, how can you not?
You've heard that Aegisthus isn't at home,
but our mother is. Don't worry that she'll ever
see my face radiant with smiles.   1310
For my long abiding hatred of her is deeply
ingrained in me, and now that I've seen you, I'll never cease
melting with tears of joy. For how can I stop,
who on this single day saw you come home both
dead and alive? And you've done something incredible to me,   1315
so that if my father were to come back to life,

1288-383 The second scene of the fourth episode. The action resumes, broken by a short inter-
        val when Electra once again bursts out in an enthusiastic expression of joy when she
        recognizes the Paedagogus as the person who had smuggled Orestes away to Phocis.
1288-300 Orestes is back to the pragmatism that characterized him in the first speech of the
        play. Without mincing words, he cautions Electra against letting her emotions run
        away with her and tells her that what he wants is information that will help him in
        the situation at hand. He is calculating, exacting in his demands, and wants a speedy
        decision and action.

I wouldn't think it a monstrous vision, but believe I saw him.
So now that you've come to me in the way you have,
command me as you wish. For had I been by myself
I wouldn't have lost out on one of two things: either   1320
a glorious liberation or a glorious death.

Orestes
Quiet now! I hear someone
coming out of the house.

Electra
Go inside, strangers,
especially since you're bringing what no one
there can repel, nor rejoice in receiving.   1325

The Paedagogus enters from the palace.

Paedagogus
You unthinking fools!
Don't you care about your lives anymore?
or have the innate sense
to realize that you're not close to deadly
perils, but in the midst of them?   1330
Why, if I hadn't been keeping watch at this doorway
for some time, your plans would have
been in the house before your persons!
But, as it is, I saw to these things in advance.
So now leave off these long speeches and   1335
these insatiate shrieks of joy, and go inside.
For delay is ruinous in such matters,
and it's high time we're done with our purpose.

1321   *a glorious liberation or a glorious death*: she would either have killed the murderers
      or died in trying.

1324-25   Electra shows surprising command of her emotions. Not only does she abruptly
      halt her joyous speech; she effects a remarkable dissimulation on the spot. Believing
      that someone is coming out of the palace, she assumes the manner of a polite hostess
      and invites Orestes and Pylades inside as though they were the Phocian emissaries
      they pretend to be.

1326   Although Electra and Orestes expect someone who lives in the palace and who might
      endanger them, it is the Paedagogus who appears. Electra, who doesn't recognize him,
      asks Orestes who he is.

1338   *high time*: The Paedagogus repeats the last statement he made to Orestes when he first
      counseled him (20-22n): that the proper time is the best for achieving victory.

Orestes

How will I find things when I go inside?

Paedagogus

Good! No one will recognize you.   1340

Orestes

You've evidently reported that I'm dead.

Paedagogus

Here you're surely among those in Hades.

Orestes

So are they happy with the news? What did they say?

Paedagogus

I'll tell you when it's all over. As things are now,
all's well as far as they're concerned, even what's not well.   1345

Electra

Who's this man, brother? Tell me, please!

Orestes

Don't you recognize him?

Electra

No! I can't even guess!

Orestes

You don't recognize the man into whose hands you gave me?

Electra

Is this the man? What are you saying?

1345   *what's not well*: may refer to Orestes being alive when Clytemnestra thinks he's dead and/ or to Clytemnestra being busy with preparing his urn for burial. In either case, Clytemnestra's illusion or busyness would keep her from suspecting the avengers' presence or plans.

1346-83 While the Paedagogus pushes to get the revenge under way, Electra slows down the deed by forcing a mini-recognition on him. After the Paedagogus calms her down, Orestes and Pylades go into the palace following a short prayer (1374-75). Electra remains and prays to Apollo, and then goes into the palace herself (1383). This is her only exit in the play. She will return to the stage shortly, after the Chorus' song ending in 1397. We may assume that the attendants enter the palace with the urn to show it to Clytemnestra.

1346   Electra's failure to recognize the Paedagogus must be reassuring, because it suggests that the royal couple will have similar difficulty recognizing Orestes after so many years.

Orestes

                              By whose hands I was secretly
conveyed to the Phocian plain, thanks to your forethought.   1350

Electra

Is this the man — the only one of many whom
I found loyal when our father was murdered?

Orestes

This is the man! Don't interrogate me with further questions.

Electra

Oh happiest of days! Oh sole savior of the house
of Agamemnon, how is it that you've come? Is it really you,   1355
who saved him and me from our many torments?
Oh most beloved hands, and you whose feet rendered
the most beloved service, how, though you had been with me
for so long, have you eluded my notice and given no sign, but killed
me with your words, though you did me the sweetest deed?   1360
Welcome, oh father! For I think I see my father.
Welcome! Know that of all living men, in one day
it was you I hated most and most loved.

Paedagogus

I think this is enough! As for the story of what happened
in between, many nights and the same number of days   1365
revolving around will make it all clear to you, Electra.
But I really must advise you two, who are all set to go,
that now is the time act. Now Clytemnestra is alone.
Now there are no men inside. If you stop now,
bear in mind that you'll have to fight them   1370
along with other men who are smarter and more numerous than they.

1362   *in one day* can refer either to the present day, when Electra hated the Paedagogus for
       bringing the news of Orestes' death and loved him after she learned that he had saved
       him, or to the distant past, when the Paedagogus took Orestes off, at which time she
       would have hated him for taking Orestes away from her and loved him for saving
       him.

1368-71 The upcoming matricide is cast in unheroic colors, as a deed to be committed with
       the least possible risk and when no men are in the house to put up a fight.

1368   *time*: The Paedagogus uses the idea of opportune time again, see 20-22n. This is
       the first time that it is explicitly said that Clytemnestra will be killed. Until now, her
       murder has only been hinted at.

Orestes

Pylades, our undertaking needs no more
speeches, but action. We must go
inside with all speed, first worshiping the statues of my
father's gods, who inhabit these portals.   1375

*The Paedagogus, Orestes, Pylades, and the attendants enter the
palace. One of the attendants carries the urn.*

Electra [*turning to the statue of Apollo, as Clytemnestra did before*]
Lord Apollo, listen to these two men with favor, and to me too,
who often stood before you sacrificing
with devoted hand from whatever I had in store.
Now, Lycean Apollo, with all that I have,
I beg, I implore you on my knees, I pray,   1380
be attentive to us, help us
to carry out our plans, and show mankind
the gods' punishment for iniquity.

Electra goes into the palace.

Chorus   *Strophe*
See how Ares,
breathing blood that breeds strife, advances.   1385
They've just gone into the house,
these inescapable hounds
hunting down evil,
so that the vision
in my mind will not long hover in suspense.   1390
For the champion of those underground   *Antistrophe*
stealthily moves into the house,

1376-83 Electra's prayer parallels Clytemnestra's in 634-59.
1384-97 The Chorus is left alone in the *orchestra*. Their short ode predicts the success of
   the undertaking.
1387 *inescapable hounds*: The Furies (112-13n) are frequently likened to hounds that track
   spilled blood (cf. Aeschylus, *Libation Bearers* 924; *Eumenides* 246-47). Orestes and
   Pylades are thus identified with the Furies, for whom Electra prayed in 112-13 and
   the Chorus foresaw coming (489-91).
1389-90 The Chorus are referring back to their vision of Justice coming in 472-502.
1391 *the champion of those underground* refers to Orestes, as indicated by 1392, which tells
   of his moving into the house. The Greek word for "champion" has legal connotations
   (e.g., advocate, defender) and is yet another instance of legal language in this play.

into the palace rich of old, with
newly-whetted blood upon his hands.
And Maia's son,   1395
Hermes, after hiding his guile in darkness,
leads him to the goal itself, and tarries no more.

Electra emerges from the palace.

Electra   *Strophe*
My dearest ladies, the men are about
to complete the deed any time now. Silence, please!

Chorus
What's happening? What are they doing now?

Electra
                                        She's adorning the urn for burial,
and the two of them are standing next to her.   1401

Chorus
Then why have you come outside?

Electra
                                        To see to it that
Aegisthus doesn't go into the house without our knowledge.

Clytemnestra
Aiai! Aiai! The house
is empty of friends and full of killers.   1405

1396 Hermes, called Crafty Hermes, is both the god who guides the souls of the dead to
      the Netherworld (111n) and a god known for his trickery. Here he acts in his double
      capacity: just as he had guided Agamemnon to the Netherworld, so he now provides
      Orestes with the trickery he needs to avenge Agamemnon's death.

1398-441 This is an antistrophic *kommos*: a song in which Electra and the Chorus sing in stanzas.
      There are probably some lines missing in the antistrophe (three lines after 1427, one
      line before 1430, and the second part of either 1431 or 1432). The gap in 1431 or 1432 is
      certain, that in the other lines is argued by some scholars. If there is indeed a gap, we may
      be missing Electra's and Orestes' last comments on their mother's death. As Kamerbeek
      (1974) observes, this loss would have a bearing on our judgment of Electra.

      Clytemnestra is murdered four lines after Electra comes out of the palace. By remov-
      ing Electra from the scene of the murder, Sophocles enables her to serve as a source
      of information about what is happening inside.

1400 In the *Iliad*, the urn containing Patroclus' ashes is said to be covered with a "thin
      veil" (23.253-54), believed to be of linen, and the urn containing Hector's ashes to be
      wrapped in soft purple robes (24.796).

1404 Clytemnestra is heard from inside the palace, just as Electra had been at the beginning
      of the play.

Electra

Someone is crying out inside. Don't you hear, friends?

Chorus

Sadly I hear what should be never heard —
and shudder.

Clytemnestra

Help! Aegisthus, where are you?

Electra

Listen, someone is crying out again!

Clytemnestra

                           Child! Oh child!   1410
Pity the one who bore you!

Electra

                         But he was never pitied by you,
nor the father who begot him.

Chorus

Oh city! Oh unhappy family! Now the fate
that has daily pursued you is dying, dying.

Clytemnestra

Aiai! I'm stabbed!

Electra

                Strike her a second time, if you have the strength! 1415

1406   *Someone is crying out inside*: Kamerbeek (1974) comments: "derisive and jeering."
       But there may also be horror in Electra's voice or numbness. The tone one attributes to
       Electra here would reflect the way one interprets her character, as well as Sophocles'
       aims in this scene.

1413-14 These lines are problematic. If we understand "family" as a collective term for the
       house of Pelops, the Chorus may be understood as saying that the curse, and the
       many troubles of the house, will come to an end with the murder of Clytemnestra.
       This view, however, seems to be contradicted by the claim in 1418-21 that the dead
       are alive and draining the blood of their murderers, which suggests that Clytemnestra
       and Aegisthus may someday wreak vengeance on those who murdered them. March's
       (2001) suggestion that "family" here might be understood as a single offspring (in
       which case the term would refer to Electra, whom the Chorus are addressing) does
       not resolve the contradiction.

1415   *Strike her a second time*: A line that still reverberates in Voltaire's *Oreste* in the
       eighteenth century and in Hugo von Hofmannstahl's *Elektra* in the twentieth century.
       See Afterlife 113-117.

Clytemnestra
Aiai! Yet again!

Electra
　　　　If only Aegisthus were here too!

Chorus
The curses are doing their work!
Those who lie underground are alive.
For those long since dead are draining the blood　　　　　1420
that flows from their murderers in recompense.

Orestes and Pylades emerge from the palace. Orestes is
carrying a bloody sword.

They're really here; a bloody hand　　　　　*Antistrophe*
drips with the sacrifice to Ares. I cannot blame them.

Electra
Orestes, how are you doing?

Orestes
　　　　　　　　In the house
all is well, if Apollo prophesized well.　　　　　1425

Electra
Did the wretched woman die?

Orestes
　　　　　　　　Fear no more;
Never again will our mother's haughty spirit dishonor you.

1419-21 The image is of the dead taking an active role in avenging their murderers. If the
　　　blood is drained in recompense, Orestes too will have to pay with his blood: the curse
　　　is not going to stop with the murder of Clytemnestra and Aegisthus. Kitto (1966)
　　　179-88 points out that there are similar cases in Sophocles where the dead reach out
　　　to kill the living (*Women of Trachis* 1159-63, *Ajax* 1025-27, *Oedipus the King* 1451-
　　　54). See 1413-14n.

1422　*They're really here*: The Chorus indicate that Orestes and Pylades have come out-
　　　side.

1425　*if Apollo prophesized well*: This clause is somewhat ambiguous. The "if" can convey
　　　either doubt (e.g., that Apollo might not have prophesized well) or conviction (the
　　　assumption that he did prophesize well). Thus, Kirkwood (1994) 241-42, n.22 sees
　　　here "a faintly ominous note" and Kamerbeek (1974) sees an expression of anxiety,
　　　while Jebb (2004) reads an expression of confidence.

Chorus

Stop! I see
Aegisthus in clear view.

Electra

Boys! Get back inside!

Orestes

Where do you see
the man?   1430

Electra

[pointing] There. He's coming this way from the outskirts of the city,
looking thrilled.

Chorus

Get out of the vestibule — quickly!
You've done the first part well; now be off to the second.

Orestes

Take heart, we'll do it!

Electra

Hurry, now, to where you want to go!   1435

Orestes

There, I'm gone. [*goes into the palace*]

Electra

I'll take care of matters here!

Chorus

It would be good
to slip some soothing words into his ear,
so he'll   1440
rush unsuspecting into his match with justice.

Aegisthus enters by one of the side entrances.

1428-29 Sophocles pushes the action without allowing the characters to think any more about
Clytemnestra's death.

Aegisthus

Which of you knows where the strangers from
Phocis are, who have reported, it is said,
that Orestes lost his life in a chariot wreck?
You, I'm asking, it is you? Yes, you, who've been   1445
so brazen in the past. I think you care most,
and are most likely to know and be able to tell me.

Electra

Of course I know! For otherwise I'd be
a stranger to the fortunes of my nearest and dearest.

Aegisthus

Then where would the foreigners be? Tell me!   1450

Electra

Inside. They've reached the house of a kind hostess.

Aegisthus

And have they actually reported that he's really dead?

Electra

More than that. They've shown proofs, not words alone.

Aegisthus

Can I see him then in plain sight?

Electra

Of course you can, but it's a rather unenviable sight.   1455

Aegisthus

Your words please me immensely, which is unusual for you.

Electra

Be pleased then if this brings you joy.

1442-507 The last part of the revenge. Aegisthus, directing his speech mainly to Electra,
asks about the Phocian strangers and orders her to open the palace doors. Orestes and
Pylades emerge from the palace as the wooden platform (*ekkyklema*) with Clytemnestra's covered corpse is wheeled out. When Aegisthus lifts the covers and discovers
Clytemnestra, he realizes that the Phocian stranger is none other than Orestes, who
makes him go back into the palace to his death.

1445-47 Aegisthus, somewhat surprisingly, does not comment on Electra's being outside. Is
he so taken by the news of Orestes' death that he ignores her violation of his commands?

1455   *unenviable sight*: Most simply, the sight would be unenviable because Orestes' body
is supposedly mangled and, therefore, upsetting to look at. More essentially, it is
unenviable because Aegisthus will be looking at the body of his wife.

Aegisthus

> I command your silence and that the palace-gates be opened
> for all the Mycenaeans and Argives to see,
> so that if any of them was once   1460
> buoyed up by empty hopes on account of this man,
> now, seeing his corpse, they may accept my bit and not
> learn wisdom under the compulsion of punishment from me.

Electra

> I've done what I had to do. For at long last
> I've learned some sense: to come to terms with those in power.   1465

> *A wheeled platform termed the* ekkyklema *is rolled out of the*
> *palace door, bearing the shrouded corpse of Clytemnestra.*
> *Orestes and Pylades emerge from the palace as the messengers*
> *who brought the news.*

Aegisthus

> Oh Zeus! I see a portent that has not appeared
> without the gods' malice. So lest there's bad luck
> in it, I'll say nothing. Lift the covering from the face, so
> that my blood relative may receive my due laments.

Orestes

> Lift it yourself! It's not for me, but for you to look   1470
> at these remains and address them lovingly.

Aegisthus

> Your advice is good and I'll follow it.
> Call Clytemnestra for me, if she's somewhere in the house.

Orestes

> She's right here; look no further.

Aegishtus [*lifting the cover from Clytemnestra's corpse*]

> Oh! What do I see?

Orestes

> Who are you afraid of? Whom don't you recognize?

1464   *I've done what I had to do*: Electra is probably referring to Aegisthus' order to open
the palace doors.

1466-67 Aegisthus, thinking Orestes dead, believes that he must have died as a consequence
of the gods' displeasure, whether because of his threats against his mother (Kells,
1973) and stepfather (Jebb, 2004), or their jealousy of his spectacular success in the
Pythian Games (Kamerbeek, 1974), assuming he heard of it.

Aegisthus
> Into whose nets have I   1475
> fallen, poor wretch that I am?

Orestes
>   Haven't you realized that for some time now, you,
> though still alive, have been bandying words with the dead.

Aegisthus
> Ah! I understand what you're saying; this must be
> none other than Orestes speaking to me!   1480

Orestes
> And you, such a seer, were deceived for so long?

Aegisthus
> I'm done for! But let me say
> a few words!

Electra
>   By the gods, don't let him to say another thing,
> brother, or spin out words at length.
> For when mortals are in the thick of trouble,   1485
> what can one who is about to die gain with time?
> No, kill him as quickly as possible, and when you've killed him,
> hand him over to such grave-diggers as he deserves,
> far from our sight. For this is my only release from
> the pains that have plagued me for so long.   1490

Orestes
> Go inside quickly! For now it's
> not a verbal match, but a struggle for your life.

Aegisthus
> Why are you leading me inside? Why, if this action is honorable
> do you need darkness and don't kill me here?

Orestes
> Don't give orders! Go to where you murdered   1495
> my father, so that you'll die in the same place.

1483-84 There is a certain irony in this request. Electra, who has been so loquacious throughout the play, pushes Orestes not to allow Aegisthus some last words.

1495-96 *where you murdered my father*: At the hearth (270n). Murder usually did not take
place onstage. It was conventional for revenge murders to be carried out at the same
place and with the same weapon as those pertaining to the original crime.

Aegisthus

Is it really necessary that this house see both
the present evils of Pelops' sons and those to come?

Orestes

Yours, at least! I'm the best prophet of that for sure.

Aegisthus

But you can't boast that your father had that skill!   1500

Orestes

You talk back too much! You are slowing down the march!
Go on!

Aegisthus

    You lead!

Orestes

        You must go first!

Aegisthus

Are you afraid I'll escape you?

Orestes

        No. So you won't be able to die as you please;
I must make sure your death will be bitter for you.
This is the punishment that should be meted out straightaway   1505
to all who would act against the law:
let them be killed! For this way there'll be fewer crimes.

*Aegisthus goes into the palace, followed by Orestes and
Pylades.*

1497-98 Although these are the words of a desperate man, they also remind the audience of
troubles to come, whether Orestes' murder of Aletes (Aegisthus' son with Clytemnestra) or his pursuit by the Furies.

1500   Aegisthus' taunt is that Agamemnon could not foresee the trap that was laid for him
when he entered his house on his return from Troy.

1502-507 Sophocles ends the play before assuring the audience that Aegisthus has been
killed.

1507   A rather brutal and overly general statement, as though Orestes has arrogated to
himself the task not only of purifying his father's house but of eradicating the evils
of the world.

Chorus
Children of Atreus, after so much
suffering you've attained freedom at last,
accomplished with today's deed!

1508-10 Because the Chorus' closing lines are so different in spirit from the rest of the play, some scholars (e.g., Ritter, 1861, 430-431) question whether they were actually authored by Sophocles; some suggest that they might have been added by Euripides. Several scholars find it unsatisfactory. Thus Hogan (1991) writes: "Though typical of closings, the generality has little point and the sense is not altogether apt." Kells (1973) calls it a "taglike" and "ironic" ending. On the other hand, March (2001) declares: "... What is emphasized here is release, freedom, triumph. To dismiss these words as a perfunctory tag, unworthy of attention, as does Kells, is inadmissible."

INTERPRETATIVE ESSAY

The plot of Sophocles' *Electra*, like that of Aeschylus' and Euripides' treatments, progresses inexorably to the revenge killings at the end of the play. Much more than those plays, however, it treats Agamemnon's murder not as an isolated act, but the source of a multitude of ills. These include the pollution that emanates from the murder of a king, cousin, and husband; the usurpation of the throne by his murderers; the sexual corruption of their adulterous affair; and the deprivations of the children — Orestes' exile and Electra's pauperization, servitude, and exclusion — that follow from the murderers' need to protect their ill-gotten gains and to prevent the retribution they deserve. Each of these ills calls for rectification, which cannot be accomplished so long as Clytemnestra and Aegisthus are on the throne.

Because of the public ramifications of Agamemnon's murder, the revenge is not only a private act to restore the avengers' personal honor and rights, but a public act required to cleanse and restore order to the polity. The Chorus, the voice of authority in Greek tragedy, refer to the revenge as an act of justice (473-76,1386-88,1423,1440-41) and never express any doubts about its morality. Orestes and Electra, unlike their namesakes in Aeschylus' and Euripides' plays, express neither trepidation nor regret (34, 1299-300, 1372-75, 1379-83, 1398-99, 1406, 1409, 1415, 1426-27). Moreover, through repeated, vivid descriptions of the brutal axe murder by both the Chorus (193-200) and the avengers (95-102, 443-46), Sophocles keeps it in the audience's mind throughout the play. Nevertheless, matricide is universally abhorrent and taboo. The tension between the necessity of the revenge and its horror creates a conundrum, which the play refuses to resolve but rather examines and re-examines from a variety of perspectives.

The Prologue: Enter the Avengers

The Prologue (1-120) introduces the avengers, in depictions that enable the audience to understand and sympathize with their motives, while raising reservations about their conduct.

Orestes is depicted as a meritorious young man, yet compromised by what he will have to do to accomplish the revenge. Returned from exile to the homeland for which he had yearned, he is on the threshold of adulthood, come to fulfill the mission to which he had been raised by his Paedagogus, the devoted slave who had taken him away to safety after his father's murder and who represents the voice of tradition and transmitter of values in the play. Overall, Orestes is shown to comport himself well. He treats the Paedagogus with the appreciation and respect due to him as his elder, albeit a slave, and as the serving man who had remained loyal to his father. Yet, as befits his station, he takes command of the situation, outlining his plans for the vengeance and assigning the Paedagogus his part in it. With due respect for the gods, he consults the oracle before embarking on his vengeance and places libations on his father's grave in keeping with Apollo's commands. His methodical and systematic presentation of the plan by which he will carry out the revenge shows a logical mind and a well-regulated temperament (38-58). His goals (67-70) — to purify the house, gain honor, and regain the wealth of which he had been robbed — would all have been viewed as admirable and noble in the son of a murdered king. His intuition that the cries coming from behind the palace doors are those of his sister (when the Paedagogus had attributed them to a serving girl, 78-81) point to the warmth and concern that he will express more explicitly in the scene where he and Electra meet face to face (1174-226).[1]

And yet, to accomplish the revenge, Orestes adopts dubious behaviors: deceit and an opportunistic attitude. His plan to carry out the vengeance using *dolos* (cunning, guile, stealth, trickery) and his justification of the means (a false report that he has died) with the outrageous generalization that "no speech that brings profit is bad" (61) are morally compromising. Yet the deceit, which is commanded by Apollo (36-37), is essential under the circumstances. Orestes is the weaker party in an uneven contest: a young man returning from exile, a stranger to the place, and marked for destruction by his powerful adversaries, who have not shown themselves to fight fairly in the past.[2] A direct frontal attack would certainly have been stupid and self-destructive.

Orestes' opportunism is revealed as he directs the Paedagogus to go into the palace to gather intelligence "when/ the opportunity arises" (39-40) and prods him with the sweeping generalization that "it's time [to act], and timing/ is man's greatest commander in every act" (75-76). It conveys

---

1 Cf. Segal (1966) 515. The counter-claim is that Orestes' leaving the scene shows an unemotional purposefulness, e.g., Winnington-Ingram (1980) 229.

2 For Apollo's command, see March (2001) 16-18 and bibliography. For the realistic and dispassionate way Orestes reacts to the situation, see Woodard (1964) 165-168, (1965) 211. Some critics, e.g., Schein (1982) 79, Kells (1973) 6-7, claim that Orestes' readiness to employ deceit and to grasp the "opportune" moment places a pall over his character and, by extension, over the morality of the vengeance.

callowness and lack of reflection. Yet seizing the moment is vital because the longer Orestes stays in Argos, the more likely he is to be discovered. Indeed, the Greek word, *kairos*, which Orestes uses in the above quoted statements, had the positive connotation of the "right" time, so that the statements may just as well bespeak prudence and a well-regulated mindset as an opportunistic one.

Orestes' deception and opportunism define the difference between the rightness of the revenge and the means that may be needed to bring it — or any moral ideal — into being.

Electra is drawn as a riveting figure, whose grief is moving but also excessive and unrestrained. She is introduced singing a lyric lament (*thrênos*) for her father, in which, beating her breasts, she bemoans his violent murder, tells of her continuing grief, and calls for vengeance (86-120).[3] The passionate grief she displays, so different from Orestes' logic and restraint, untainted by his pragmatic opportunism, provides the emotional rationale for the revenge.[4] Yet, repeated nightly since Agamemnon's death almost a decade earlier and accompanied by self-mutilation (Electra beats her breasts till they bleed), her lament bears the marks of pathological grief: intense, all consuming, and unabated by time. It is also a willed lament, which she explicitly refuses to cease (104), and a public lament, made outside the palace doors (108-09). We thus see Electra wallowing in her grief and using it to keep her father's murder alive in the public mind.

In creating his heroine, Sophocles drew on the ancient Greek stereotypes of the irrational woman and witch. Praying for vengeance, Electra calls not on the Olympic gods (e.g., Zeus or Apollo), but, much like Euripides' Medea, on the darker powers: Hermes of the underworld, Curse, and the Furies (111-12). This presentation will allow the predominantly male audience of the tragedies both to revel in the idealism and extremism of the passionate heroine and to dismiss her speeches as the ravings of an overwrought — and dangerous — female.

In Evil Straits

Electra's confrontations with the Chorus in the first episode and with her sister Chrysothemis in the second and third episodes deal less with the revenge as such than with the broader philosophical question of

---

3 On the traditional lament, see Alexiou (2002) 3-23. Pictorial evidence shows mourning figures lacerating their necks, beating their heads, and tearing out their hair. Aeschylus' Electra prays for revenge and for help from Zeus and Agamemnon (*Libation Bearers* 332-39, 363-71, 394-99, 462, 471-78, 500-509).

4 On Orestes and Electra as opposites, see Woodard (1964) and (1965).

what stand to take in face of the inevitable corruption and injustice of the world, as represented by the rule of Agamemnon's adulterous murderers. This question is much the same as that with which Sophocles grapples in *Antigone* and *Philoctetes.*

Electra is drawn as the rebel and revolutionary, the intrepid fighter for justice, who takes an absolute and unyielding position in the face of life's ills. The Chorus and Chrysothemis, presenting the non-heroic stance of ordinary persons, urge moderation and compromise — the Chorus for the sake of psychological survival, Chrysothemis for the sake of physical survival and well-being. Their common sense positions are affirmations of life against the pull toward death that characterizes Electra's stance, as she melts (122, 282), "wastes away" (304, 819, 836, 1181), and exhausts herself in her unrelenting anger, grief, and waiting for Orestes. Electra has so little sense of self-preservation that she responds to Chrysothemis' warning that Aegisthus plans to bury her alive if she does not hold her tongue with the defiant reply, "So let him come as soon as he can, if this is what he wants to do" (387). Yet, as the play presents her *contras*, their claims do not clearly outweigh Electra's counterclaims, nor hers, theirs.

Confrontation with the Chorus

Electra's confrontation with the Chorus focuses on the unremitting intensity of her grief and rage. The Chorus are depicted as women of unquestionable good will, who come to console Electra and to try to pull her out of her misery with well-meant, reasonable counsels.[5] They point out the destructiveness (140-42) of Electra's "insatiable" and "intractable" grief, her bizarre yearning for her suffering (140-44), and her own input into her troubles (215-19). Their main recommendations are that she "neither be overly vexed with those you hate/ nor entirely forget them" (177-78) and that she let time assuage her sorrow (179).

Their well-meant, sensible arguments, however, consist largely of unconvincing platitudes and irrelevancies. Of course they are correct in pointing out that neither Electra's lamentations nor her prayers will bring Agamemnon back to life (137-39). But since when do grief, mourning, and prayer have to yield concrete outcomes to be valid? Their observation that Electra is not the only one who suffers grief (153-54) is similarly incontrovertible. But how many people's fathers were murdered by their mothers? And does the fact that other people suffer grief ameliorate the intensity of one's own? The Chorus' optimistic assurance that Zeus

---

5 That the Chorus never criticize the revenge indicates to many scholars that Sophocles does not either, e.g., March (1996), (2001) 17-18.

"watches over and rules everything" (175) raises the question of where he was when Agamemnon was murdered, Orestes forced to live in exile, and Electra prevented from marrying and turned into a servant in her father's home. Their claim that time "is an easy god" (179) is belied by Electra's childlessness, although, as is implied, her time for marriage and childbearing has passed.

Electra's position is given more weight than the Chorus'. Her arguments have substance and are free of platitudes and irrelevancies. She makes her arguments twice, once in the lyric dialogue with the Chorus and again in an uninterrupted fifty-six line spoken monologue (254-309). This reinforces them. Yet, here too the text causes us to pause and wonder.

The core of Electra's argument is that the situation is untenable and allows for no other response than her unattenuated grief and persistent, obdurate lamentation: "[H]ow can any well-born woman/ not act this way when she sees the sufferings of her/ father's house...?" (257-59). Underpinning this rhetorical question is the cultural expectation in Sophocles' Athens that high-born individuals, as Electra was, act in "noble" ways that reflect the "nobility" of their birth and character. In her exchanges with the Chorus, Electra offers cogent and emotionally powerful supports for this claim.

Describing her current circumstances, she paints a vivid and moving picture of her deprivation and abuse by her father's murderers, and her loneliness, frustration, and vulnerability after they prevented her from marrying lest her children grow up to avenge Agamemnon's murder. In a particularly moving depiction, she tells how she has been turned into an ill-treated, badly dressed servant, who cleans her father's rooms and "stand[s] at empty tables" (189-93) in what had been her father's home. Her mother, she says, vilifies her (289), wishes her dead (291), and reproaches her for having removed Orestes out of harm's way (295-97).

She also provides a number of moral arguments for her persistent lamentation. One is the moral imperative to continue her lamentations so as to honor her father. "Only a simpleton forgets/ parents who died piteously" (145-46), Electra declares. "How can it be good to neglect the dead?/ To what human being is this natural?" (237-38) she challenges. Another is the ongoing affront of the royal couple's conduct to public decency. Her mother, she says, celebrates her father's death in a monthly festival (277-81) and sleeps with his murderer (271-73), and Aegisthus sits on her father's throne, wears his clothes, pours libations at the hearth where he killed him, and sleeps in his bed (266-74). A third is that if the murderers go unpunished, the entire fabric of public order will collapse, as "shame and respect for law/ will forsake all mortals" (245-50).

These claims are unassailable. How can one deny that Electra would be less miserable if she had been permitted to live a more fulfilled life with a husband and children? The moral obligation to remember and honor a parent is axiomatic. The outrageous conduct of the royal couple surely cannot be allowed to continue. And the notion that if murder goes unpunished there will be nothing to inhibit crime has its validity today.

In the course of the encounter, in three gnomic pronouncements of what may be termed the argument of necessity, she reiterates her core claim that no other response was open to her. The first, toward the end of the lyric dialogue, is that "Dreadful deeds forced me to dreadful deeds" (221). The other two come at the beginning and end of her monologue, where she states that "unlawful force compels" (256) her to her grief and lamentations, and that "…in evil straits/ one's conduct must be evil too" (308-309). These are forceful assertions that convey Electra's sense of personal compulsion and raise the "dreadful," extreme, and "evil" acts she will commit to a moral imperative.

Yet Electra's statements also contain discordant notes, which may cause one to pause and consider her position. In the exchange with the Chorus, the most grating is perhaps Electra's assertion of emotional affinity with Procne ("that mournful bird") and Niobe, two mythical women who grieved incessantly for their deceased children:

> … It is that mournful bird that suits my mind,
> the bird who is distraught by grief, the messenger of Zeus,
> who forever laments Itys! Itys!
> Oh, you too, all-suffering,
> Niobe, to me you're a goddess,
> you who forever shed tears
> in your rocky grave.   (147-52)

This assertion conveys and gives grandeur to the intense grief and perpetual mourning that Electra shares with these mythical figures. As Sophocles' audience well knew, however, both these figures were responsible for their children's deaths. Procne killed her son Itys and served his flesh to her husband, Tereus, in revenge for his rape and mutilation of her sister Philomela. Niobe's children were killed by the goddess Leto after Niobe bragged that she had more children than the goddess. Electra's expression of affinity thus highlights the murderous and destructive aspect of her grief, as well as its self-perpetuation and futility, since these figures never cease to mourn. It also underscores the horror of revenge.

Other claims she makes will lose something of their power in retrospect, when the high-minded principles declared in the largely intellectual debate with the Chorus can be compared with their application in actual situations. In her confrontation with Chrysothemis, Electra declares that if the price for the good things of life is ceasing her lamentations, she willingly foregoes them (352-54) and pours scorn on her sister's comfortable lifestyle (361-65). But if this is how she feels, why does she complain so bitterly about her deprivations and mistreatment? Her later admission to Chrysothemis that the purpose of her lamentations, carried out in public outside the palace doors, is to "nettle them [the royal couple] so as to confer honor on the dead" (355) gives her laments a political cast. One wonders whether she would not have found a quieter and less provocative way of honoring her father if her lamentations had not had the purpose of annoying and embarrassing Clytemnestra and Aegisthus.

In particular, her repeated statements of necessity raise profound questions. Made in conjunction with her many assertions that she *will not* cease her lamentations (103-106, 132-33, 147-52, 224-25, 231-32), they capture the strong sense that characterizes many idealistic, principled individuals who sacrifice themselves to a cause: that they cannot act any differently than the way they believe they should. But they also confound *will not* with *cannot* and deny the choices that Electra makes in her response to life's evils and ills.

In her confrontations with her mother, Electra uses variants of the argument to divest herself of responsibility for her actions. Drawing on notions of heredity,[6] she blames her mother for her own character flaws and misconduct:

...Say that I'm disloyal or sharp tongued, or utterly
without shame. For if by nature I'm accomplished in any of these
things, then I'm surely not putting your nature to shame. (607-609)

A few lines later, she admits that she is behaving "unreasonably and contrary/ to my nature" (618-19), but continues to blame her mother: "But your enmity/ and your actions force me to behave like this against my will./ For ugly deeds are taught by ugly deeds" (619-21). Thus applied to her mother's face and with specific reference to her mother's actions, the argument from necessity loses its grandeur.

Before bidding the Chorus to leave her to her grief, Electra asks them whether persons "whose wisdom is attuned to the moment," as theirs is, "can give me useful advice?" (226-28). The question is a powerful expression of Electra's and the play's deep skepticism regarding the utility of conventional wisdom, such as the Chorus offer, in the face of life's troubles. The Chorus,

---

6 On Electra's similarity to her mother, see Segal (1966) 505-21, 525-526.

for their part, cease to dispute Electra and admit that they might give her more support (314). Yet Electra does not come out clearly on top. The claims on both sides are too flawed to fully accept, but also too strong to fully reject.

The Sisters' Quarrels

Chrysothemis appears in neither Aeschylus' nor Euripides' treatments of the myth. She is the conventional, timid sister who, like Ismene in *Antigone*, serves as a foil to the play's rebellious, principled heroine. Each sister urges the other to "think rightly" while meaning completely different things by the term: Electra means think morally (346); Chrysothemis, think sensibly (394, 890, 1038, cf. 384). In the debate with the Chorus, the opposing positions were judged largely by the cogency of the arguments. The sisters' confrontations move the debate to a personal plane, in which their positions are reflected in their conduct and interactions.[7]

Chrysothemis' advice to Electra is to curb her "foolish anger" (331) and to "sail with lowered sail" (335) — that is to emulate her own restraint, circumspection, and submission to superior power. In reward, Chrysothemis is allowed the pleasures of life — good food, good clothes, and civil treatment — that are denied to Electra, as well as greater freedom of movement than Electra is permitted. For this, Electra berates Chrysothemis for disloyalty to their father, hypocrisy (for hating the royal couple only in "words" and not in "deeds"),[8] and cowardice (351). It is hard to deny the appeal of Electra's idealism over her sister's conventionality and pragmatism, and not to thrill at her courage, sacrifice, and moral conviction. Hers is the appeal of the fighter for justice and the appeal, too, of a black and white view of reality, free of ambivalence, nuance, and ambiguity.

Chrysothemis, however, is shown to be the kinder, more caring, more accommodating sister. Although she comes on stage berating Electra rather sharply for being outdoors, it soon becomes apparent that she has her sister's good in mind. She has come to warn her of Aegisthus' and Clytemnestra's plans to entomb her alive if she persists in openly reviling them. She cautions Electra to hold her tongue even though her only reward for doing so is Electra's scorn. Moreover, timid as she is, she musters the courage to oppose her mother surreptitiously, by agreeing to Electra's demand that she exchange the libation offerings Clytemnestra had given her to place on Agamemnon's grave with offerings of their own (431-63).

---

7 See Winnington-Ingram (1980) 232-242.

8 On the interplay between words and deeds, see Hartigan (1996) 85-88, Minadeo (1967), Woodard (1966).

Viewed against Chrysothemis' kindness, concern, and accommodation, Electra's vaunted moral superiority rings overbearing and simplistic. Her expression of contempt for the good life that Chrysothemis enjoys, as she wishes her "a sumptuous table" and a "life overflow[ing] with abundance" (361-62), is unnecessarily sarcastic. Her assertion, after Chrysothemis warns her of Aegisthus' designs, that she would like nothing better than "[t]o escape as far as possible from you people" (391) shows her utter lack of appreciation for Chrysothemis' effort and concern.

In their second encounter, after the Paedagogus' announcement of Orestes' death, Electra emerges as manipulative and out of touch with reality, as she tries to persuade Chrysothemis to join her in avenging their father's murder on their own. Her opening words play on the emotional bond and obligations that sisters are supposed to have for one another:

But now that he's gone, I count on you
not to shrink from killing, along with me, your sister, the man
who by his own hand murdered our father:
Aegisthus. I mustn't keep secrets from you anymore.   (954-57)

This is the first time in the play that Electra, who had not previously expressed any warmth toward Chrysothemis, calls her "sister." Moreover, even though it is clear that Electra regards her mother as a full partner in Agamemnon's murder (97-99, 205-206, 585-88), she names Aegisthus as the sole target of their revenge. Unless she is unaware of her true intentions, which seems unlikely after her confrontation with her mother in the previous scene, it is hard to escape the impression that she is trying to keep the horror of her intended matricide from Chrysothemis.[9] This omission casts doubt on the candor of Electra's declaration that she must keep no more secrets from her (957).

Electra's detachment from reality is evident in her fanciful vision of the outcome of the scheme (977-85). All the denizens of the place, citizens and foreigners alike, will greet them with praise as sisters who saved their father's house without concern for their own lives, Electra declares. At every public gathering, people will tell one another that they should love, honor, and revere the sisters for their bravery. Her dead father and supposedly dead brother may indeed praise Chrysothemis' piety, and it is not impossible that people will consider her a "free woman" (970). But will a woman who killed

---

9 Scholars have explained Electra's not mentioning her mother as a target of her revenge in three ways: as an unconscious act, which serves to keep her true intentions not only from Chrysothemis but also from herself; as one of the many means Sophocles uses to suppress all mention of matricide in the play; and as indicative that Clytemnestra is not part of Electra's plan. For bibliography, see Macleod (2001) 141 n. 7.

be viewed as a desirable wife and find a "worthy marriage"? And will it be "fame"—or notoriety—that she will win by participating in a murder? Even if Electra is correct in her claim that people admire quality (972), fame for heroic acts was deemed a masculine virtue in ancient Greece.[10] Electra is so out of touch that she refuses even to consider the possibility that the attempt may fail. Dismissing Chrysothemis' warnings that they may be caught and die by slow torture (997-1008), she determines to proceed with the scheme on her own (1017-20). This decision shows courage, but when Electra replies to Chrysothemis' nuanced observation that there are times when being right brings harm with the statement, "I don't want to live by such laws" (1043), we recognize the ideologue's refusal to accept any reality that does not accord with her ideology.

Nonetheless, Sophocles does not permit us to take Chrysothemis as a role model. Electra's criticisms stick: Chrysothemis is afraid of power, does not stand with her father against Aegisthus and her mother, and does not act openly on her dislike of them. She never even tries to refute the charges. The text lets us understand that the benefits of Chrysothemis' pragmatic acquiescence are not all that she claims they are. Chrysothemis admits to Electra that "justice isn't in the course I recommend,/ but in the course you've chosen" (338-39). Her justification for her stance — "to live/ a free person, I must heed those in power in everything" (339-40) — is self-contradictory. How can a person who must obey in all things be free? And for all that she urges Electra to bow to power, she admits that she would actually prefer to speak her mind: "if/ I had the strength, I'd show them what I think of them" (333-34).

Like the Chorus, Chrysothemis proves unequal to the challenge posed by the murderers' unjust rule. Electra's declaration that she will never ask her for help again, "since/ there's no sense in chasing after nothing" (1052-54) resonates, much as her earlier rejection of the Chorus' conventional wisdom had. Indeed, at the end of the second encounter, the Chorus come out in favor of Electra. They intimate that Chrysothemis has betrayed her, paint her as fighting a lonely and noble battle for her honor, suggest that she is the better daughter, and praise her piety in following nature's laws (1058-97). And yet, much like the altercation with the Chorus, the confrontation between the sisters also suggests that neither position — neither choosing courage, heroism, and justice despite the risk of suffering and death, nor opting for moderation, caution, good sense, and life — is entirely satisfactory.

---

10 An Athenian audience would have recognized Electra's words as referring to persons who killed tyrants (Juffras, 1991).

The Revenge

The issue of the revenge itself is dealt with more directly in the depiction of Clytemnestra in the second episode and in the juxtaposition of the recognition scene in the fourth episode and the vengeance in the fifth.

Does Clytemnestra Deserve to Die?

Among the purposes of the episode with Clytemnestra is to enable the audience to consider whether she deserves to die at her children's hands. The question is addressed in two ways.

The first is a debate, in the debate (*agôn*) between mother and daughter (516-633), on the justice of Clytemnestra's revenge killing of Agamemnon. The debate is underpinned by the twin premises that "just" murders are not to be punished but that "unjust" murders are. Intent on proving the justice of her revenge killing of Agamemnon, Clytemnestra avers that "Justice took him, not I alone" (528) and presents Agamemnon as a man who deserved to die: a hard-hearted, unthinking and malicious father who no longer loved Iphigenia and sacrificed her for the benefit of Menelaus and the Greeks.

Yet, even before we hear Electra's rebuttal, her argument is weakened by her legalistic and rights-based language and her egotistical and proprietary view of Iphigenia. The Argives, she declares, had no "right to kill my daughter, having no share in her" (536), and Agamemnon "killed what was mine and had no intention of paying for it" (538). Agamemnon, as Clytemnestra draws him, had merely sired Iphigenia and not endured the pains of childbirth as she had, and thus had no right to take the girl from her (533-34). With this account, her murder of Agamemnon becomes retaliation for the loss of valuable property more than retribution for the loss of a loved daughter. Indeed, she expresses no love for Iphigenia or grief over her loss.

Electra presents the sacrifice (563-76) as the "price" that the goddess Artemis exacted as "redress" for the stag that Agamemnon had killed in her sacred grove. As she presents it, he did not make the sacrifice lightly, but only under the most "severe constraint" (575). Until he performed the sacrifice, the entire Greek army was stranded at Aulis, unable either to proceed to Troy or to return home (573-74). Electra's account is a fuller rendition of the known myth than Clytemnestra's and brings out the terrible choice Agamemnon had to make between the life of his daughter and the lives of the entire Greek army. Yet it is marred by the same coldness as Clytemnestra had shown. Electra does not mention Iphigenia by name, and expresses no sadness that she was killed in the prime of youth.

Moreover, Sophocles throws into confusion the notion that unjust murders require punishment, by having Electra argue that justice is not grounds for revenge and does not make it right. Electra calls the murder of Agamemnon "shameful... whether it was justly done or not" (559-60). She demands to know "by what law" her father had to die, even if he had sacrificed Iphigenia to help Menelaus – that is, in an unjust cause (578-79). And she warns her mother against taking "a life for a life," as "you would be the first to die, if you got your just deserts" (582-83). These claims, made by an overwrought (female) character in the heat of argument, need not reflect the authorial view, as some critics assume. They do, however, draw Electra as a fanatic so focused on her own point of view that she will say anything to defend it without realizing its implications: namely, that it undermines the moral validity of her own pursuit of vengeance.[11]

The debate thus ends inconclusively: Clytemnestra does not manage to convince us that she does not deserve to die, but Electra raises questions about whether this gives her and her brother the right to kill their mother.

The second way the episode addresses the question is by inviting the audience to consider whether Clytemnestra is a "true mother." If she can be cast as a "false" mother, who does not treat her children with the love and care of a real mother, then their killing her is not quite matricide. Earlier in the play, the Chorus had urged Electra to accept their advice as that of a "loyal mother" (233), implying that they, not Clytemnestra, had a mother's love and concern for her. Electra, telling of her rancorous relationship with Clytemnestra, questioned whether "one can/ call her a mother" (273-74). In the *agôn*, Electra paints her as an unworthy mother ("less a mother than a ruler" (597) who cast off and mistreated Electra and her brother in favor of the children she bore to Aegisthus (585-609).

But these are third-party descriptions. In the second part of the episode, Sophocles allows the audience to decide for themselves. The first direct intimation comes in Clytemnestra's prayer to Apollo, following her dream presaging the vengeance. In the dream, Agamemnon had returned to life and planted his scepter next to the hearth where he had been murdered, and the "leafy shoot" that sprouted from it overshadowed all the land (420-23). Terrified, Clytemnestra prays to Apollo to make the dream's ill tidings rebound on her enemies and to allow her to continue to enjoy her comfortable life in the company of her friends and of "those of my children who/ harbor no ill will toward me or a bitter grudge" (653-54). She couches her prayer in "veiled" language, since Electra is in hearing distance, and ends it with a silent entreaty: "As for the rest, about which I'm silent,/ I trust that you, being a god, know it full well" (657-58). Since the ancient Greeks

---

11 For Electra's failure to see the implications of her argument, see Winnington-Ingram (1980) 22-221; Gellie (1972) 115 cf. 110; Kells (1973) 582f, Ringer (1998) 159.

prayed aloud and viewed requests made in silence as indicative of sinister intent, the spectators can think the worst: that Clytemnestra is praying for harm to come to Orestes, the "leafy shoot" of Agamemnon's scepter, which threatened to take over the land.

The intimations become more explicit with the arrival of the Paedagogus. Clytemnestra does not object to the Paedagogus' description of Orestes' death as "glad news" (666-67) and shows herself callous to Electra's distress, telling the Paedagogus not to pay any attention to her (675) and snapping at Electra to mind her own business (678).

After the Paedagogus describes Orestes' death, Clytemnestra experiences a moment of mixed feelings, in which her sense of good fortune is attenuated by maternal sorrow for her son's death:

> Oh Zeus! What am I to say about this? That it's a piece of
>   good luck?
> That it's terrible but welcome? It's a sad thing
> to save my life through my own misfortunes.   (766-68)

The moment, however, is brief, and Clytemnestra soon reverts to her characteristic egotism. Assuring the Paedagogus that his visit has not been in vain if he brought proofs of Orestes' death, she goes on to malign her son. She complains that Orestes abandoned her and never returned to visit (775-77), though his life in the palace was clearly in danger. She blames him for charging her with his father's murder (778), when the charge is correct. And she tells Electra that he is well off "as he is" (791) — which she believes is dead!

Yet even as the scene confirms that Clytemnestra is an egotistical woman who places her own interests above her children's very lives, it does not entirely deprive her of all sympathy. There is the brief moment of motherly feeling, which the audience may remember when she is being murdered. Electra, with her unmitigated railing and reproaches, could test any mother's patience. And Clytemnestra's terror of the vengeance hanging over her head so that "neither by night nor day could sweet sleep/ shelter me, but from moment to moment/ I always lived in fear of death" (780-82) is moving and convincing. When, believing Orestes dead, she tells the Paedagogus that she is finally "freed of my fear/ of him and of this girl [Electra]" (783-84), her relief is palpable and understandable.

Whether her children's hostility and the threat they pose to her life justify her behavior toward them is another matter. The episode raises, but does not answer, the question of what sacrifices a mother should make for her children. Should she be expected to sacrifice her happiness? her pleasure and fecundity as a woman? her life? Is a woman who will not make these sacrifices not a "true" mother?[12] The audiences of the tragic performances of Classical times may well have believed that she was not, and probably many modern viewers and readers would agree. Still, the question is there — nagging and discomforting us as the revenge moves toward its fulfillment.

Rebirth, Reunion, and Revenge

Aeschylus and Euripides placed the so-called "recognition scene" between brother and sister early in their plays and separated it by several episodes from the vengeance at the end. Sophocles, in contrast, defers the recognition to nearly the end of his play and makes it the immediate antecedent of the vengeance. This creates an unlikely but meaningful connection between the joyous and life-affirming reunion of brother and sister and the gruesomely depicted revenge that follows it.

The recognition scene presents an ecstatic turnabout from the division, conflict, and distress that marked the preceding episodes, as Electra and Orestes are symbolically reborn[13] and reunited both physically and emotionally. The episode opens with Orestes and Electra symbolically dead: Orestes because Electra and the Chorus believe him to be, Electra because she feels that with her brother's demise, "I've also died" (1152). Their rebirth begins with Electra's lament for him (1126-1170). This lament is more restrained than that she had sung for her father at the beginning of the play (86-120). It is spoken rather than sung and there is no breast-beating or laceration of the flesh. Yet it is an intensely moving dirge. Cradling the urn that she believes holds Orestes' ashes, Electra emphasizes the emptiness, lightness, and nothingness that remain after death and contrasts this with the full-bodied person she had loved and with the heaviness of her grief. Everything in the lament conveys the intensity of her pain: from her recollections of the "resplendent" child that Orestes had been and the pleasure she had taken in nurturing him, to her sense of having died and her wish to join Orestes in death, "for the dead...no longer suffer pain" (1130, 1170).

The loss is all the more acute because the lines place Electra in the closest possible relation to Orestes: both his favorite sister ("the one you always called 'sister'," 1148) and his true mother: the urn she cradles would have been about the size of an infant. Her account of having nurtured Orestes and of rescuing him from murder when he was a small child makes her,

---

12 Aristotle, *Nicomachean Ethics* 1159a 26-33 says that a mother's love is especially valuable because it does not derive from self-interest.

13 See Segal (1966) 516-517, for the life/death inversions in the play.

not Clytemnestra, the person who gave him life and care. "You were never/ more loved by your mother than by me" (1145-46), she declares. Orestes returns her love. He does not use the word "love," but acts the emotion, albeit in his characteristically restrained way. At Electra's moving lament for him, he loses his command of his tongue (1175) and recognizes her as his sister (1177). In the following lines he expresses his sympathy for her "misfortune" (1179), her "wasted" form, her unwedded state, and her "tribulations" (1181-87). He elicits information about her life with Agamemnon's murderers and how they forced her into servitude. It is his statement of the natural, intuitive sympathy he felt, even before he saw her — "I'm the only one who's come feeling pain for your afflictions" (1201) — that leads Electra to realize that he is a "kinsman" (1202). His sympathy for her pain is born of his love, and it is the same love that leads him to reveal himself to her (after ascertaining that the women in the Chorus can be trusted), despite the risk of detection this entails.

The recognition is cast as a rebirth, which is accomplished when Orestes takes from Electra the urn that symbolizes his death.[14] Before revealing his identity, Orestes assures Electra that it's "not right" (1211) for her to mourn, "inappropriate" (1213) for her to speak of him as dead, and that "a living person doesn't have a grave" (1219). The rebirth is completed when Orestes assures Electra that her brother is alive "If there's life in me" (1221). The rebirth is accompanied by their coming together after years of separation. In the prologue, each had occupied the stage separately, unaware of the other's presence, and in depictions so contrasted that each appeared to be only half a person. In the fourth episode, they join in an embrace and then move to cooperate with one another so that they will be able to act together with a single purpose.

Their union is emphasized in the three pairs of half-lines that express their joy at finally coming together:

Electra
　　Most joyous day!
Orestes
　　　　　　　　Most joyous, I agree.
Electra
　　O voice! You've come!
Orestes
　　　　　　　　Ask no further.

---

14 Cf. Burnett (1998) 129.

Electra
Am I holding you in my arms?
Orestes
So may you hold me always!

(1224-26)

The construction of the lines, with Electra taking the first half of each and Orestes picking up her statement in the second half (*antilabê*), mimics the reunion of the long separated siblings. Their embrace at the end is a visible image of their joining.

Their union survives, and is even augmented in the tension that arises when Orestes realizes that they are putting themselves at risk by speaking loudly within hearing of the palace. Superficially, they seem to move apart when Orestes repeatedly interrupts Electra's highly emotional ode of joy at their reunion (1232-87) with spoken warnings to lower her voice or to stop speaking altogether. The difference in their meters highlights the difference between Orestes' calculating logic and Electra's unbridled passion.[15]

Yet closer analysis shows Orestes' sensitivity toward his sister and Electra's yielding to her brother. Orestes' first admonitions are moderate in tone. He tells her to "hush" (1236, 1238) and reminds her that the women in the palace, whom Electra does not deem worth fearing, may be dangerous, as "there's Ares/ in women too" (1243-44). His admonitions become harsher when she fails to heed him. Then, he tersely cautions her not to speak of their past sorrows until "the situation calls for it" (1251-52) and, more sharply, warns her to "safeguard your freedom ... by not wanting to talk at length when the time isn't right" (1257-59). Even so, his next admonition ("I'm loath to curb your jubilation, but I fear/ you're overcome by too much joy" 1271-72) shows understanding and acceptance of his sister's feelings. It is only when he becomes exasperated with her failure to appreciate the mortal danger they are in that he cuts her off rudely ("Spare me the verbiage." 1288) and commands her to tell him only what he needs to know so that they can carry out the vengeance (1288-95).

Electra also moves toward Orestes. Following his reprimand in lines 1288-95, she agrees without demurring to do as he says: "Well, my brother! Whatever suits you/ will suit me too, because it's/ from you I've taken all my joy" (1301-303); and she further assures him that her mother will never "see my face radiant with smiles" (1310). Coming from a woman who, until this point in the play, has not agreed to do anything that anyone asked of

15 Winnington-Ingram (1980) 229; Roisman (2000) 190-199.

her and, furthermore, who has shown neither the willingness nor ability to control her emotions, these are significant concessions.

The rebirth, love, and union dramatized in this episode serve as a foundation for the vengeance, but do not lend their joy to it. Instead, the vengeance, dramatized in all its horror and brutality, becomes a shocking falling off from its high peaks.

The vengeance is constructed as justice attained. In their ode preceding the fifth episode, the Chorus hail Orestes as a "champion" (1391) of the dead. In the episode itself, they follow the action with interest (1399,1402), comment approvingly as it progresses (1418-23), warn Electra of Aegisthus' approach (1428-29), and advise her to greet Aegisthus nicely so that "he'll/ rush unsuspecting into his match with justice" (1440-41). Both Clytemnestra and Aegisthus are presented as getting no less than they deserve. Orestes kills his mother just when she is preparing to bury the urn that she believes holds his ashes, and he confronts Aegisthus soon after the latter's naked display of satisfaction at his, Orestes', supposed death (1458-63).

AFTERLIFE

Sophocles' *Electra* has left a rich legacy.[1] Most obviously, there have been countless translations and performances of translations over the centuries, in numerous countries and languages. Although these stick fairly closely to the Sophoclean text, they involve interpretation, so we can assume variations in their presentations of the characters and in the themes and "messages" they emphasize. Nonetheless, they all aim at fidelity to the original.

Further afield are adaptations, whose authors use Sophocles' text for their own purposes.[2] Some announce their Sophoclean patrimony, even as they freely incorporate elements from Aeschylus' and Euripides' versions as well. The adaptations differ widely in their fidelity to the original text and the uses to which they put it. Finally, we can observe the development and application of concepts that may be traced back to Sophocles' treatment of the story. This chapter will discuss key adaptations and some works that apply a conception of Electra which may be traceable to Sophocles' play. A major criterion of selection was my ability to access the texts, which restricts the discussion to published works available in English.

Adaptations

Voltaire, **Oreste** *(1750)*

Among the earliest modern adaptations of Sophocles' *Electra* is Voltaire's *Oreste*, first performed in Paris 1750. It was written against the

---

1   The first surviving translation is by the Latin poet Atilius. An excerpt from this transla-tion was sung at Julius Caesar's funeral in 44 BCE.

2   On performances of Sophocles' *Electra* and/or its adaptations in commercial theaters, see Hartigan (1995) 20-35, for the United States; Flashar (1991) passim, for Germany; Hall and Macintosh (2005) 152-182, 374, 379, 385, 551, for the United Kingdom; Lloyd (2005) 131-132, for Greece; and Dominik (2007) 120-121, for South Africa. In Greece and South Africa, the adaptations have had a strongly political cast. Hartigan suggests that Sophocles' play may have been performed more often than Euripides' because it offers an illustration "of a way to endure hardship, to remain true to one's cause in the face of adversity, to be ready to act at whatever cost," as well as because of the appeal of the role of Electra to many actresses (25).

background of a revival of interest in classical Greek theater. Of the three versions of the myth, Sophocles' was the most highly regarded at the time; two other French playwrights had already adapted it to the stage. Voltaire acknowledges his debt to Sophocles in his "Dedicatory Letters to the Duchess of Maine," which precedes his text, and his adaptation follows the plot of Sophocles' play more closely than any of the other adaptations to be discussed in this chapter. Yet, like other French playwrights of his day Voltaire tried to adapt the classical Greek tragedy to the proclivities of his age. His *Oreste* was one of numerous plays in a project of such adaptations aimed at "improving" on the originals — revising the Greek tragedies as the eighteenth century authors believed they should have been written.

The main "improvement" was the elimination of the darker elements of Sophocles' play, in keeping with contemporary notions that the tragic hero must be good and that classical drama was essentially a moral medium. Thus, basing himself on Clytemnestra's statement in lines 770-71 ("It is a wondrous thing to give birth. For even/ when you're treated badly, you can't hate your own children"), Voltaire transformed Sophocles' egotistical figure, who preferred her own life to the lives of her children, into a "true" mother who does her best to protect Electra and Orestes from Aegisthus' anger.[3] He also made her a dutiful wife, who tries to protect Aegisthus from Orestes' murderous intentions – and dies in the attempt.

Electra underwent an equally radical transformation. Gone are the irrationality, obsessive mourning, and driving rage of her Sophoclean namesake. In their place Voltaire endowed her with a genteel, feminine sadness, and the new ability to understand and forgive her mother. He left her only enough hatred to channel against Aegisthus, who, depicted as a cruel tyrant and undisputed villain, is the only character in the play to retain his Sophoclean flaws. Throughout most of the play, mother and daughter are reconciled. The only exception is a brief scene in which they quarrel over Aegisthus' intention to marry Electra off to a nephew so as to prevent her from acting against him.

Orestes was turned into a sentimental young hero, adored by his people. There is no sign of the abrasive practicality and opportunism of Sophocles' figure. Emphasis is placed on his brotherly sorrow as he sees Electra suffering in the belief that he is dead. His sorrow is so intense that he reveals himself to her prematurely, precipitating his capture by Aegisthus.

---

3 Although Voltaire's principal source for *Oreste* was Sophocles' *Electra*, he borrows from Euripides for his depictions of Clytemnestra and Orestes. For discussion of Voltaire's sources, influences, changes and additions, see Jory's (1992) critical edition of *Oreste*.

In contrast to the Sophoclean character, but consistent with Euripides', he experiences pangs of conscience at having killed his mother.

Voltaire, like the French writers who preceded him, also eliminated the intentional matricide as too "atrocious" to include. (His Orestes kills his mother accidentally [as she begs him to spare Aegisthus' life], in an act that is ascribed to fate.) With this change, Voltaire removed the key motive for the action in Sophocles' play, the moral dilemma at its heart, and the connection in Greek thought between fate and character.

With the moral dilemma gone, there was no longer any need for the contemplative, philosophical concerns of Sophocles' play. Voltaire removed them, along with the Sophoclean Chorus, which had raised them. Pylades, however, is given a voice and becomes the confidante figure that was part of most French tragedies of this period.

The removal of the matricidal intention required Voltaire to alter Sophocles' plot, which was driven by this intention. His *Oreste* traces the progress of Orestes' plan to kill Aegisthus, Aegisthus' discovery and capture of Orestes, and Orestes' escape from captivity with the help of the palace guards and the support of the population. Within this action, there are many sentimental moments, in which Clytemnestra, Electra, and Orestes are given the opportunity to show they are persons of feeling. Essentially, however, the change turns Voltaire's play into an "action" play with political overtones that anticipate the French revolution some forty years later.

Voltaire's adaptation retained the Greek setting, characters, and the main incidents of Sophocles' play, as well as many of the lines, but not the spirit of the original. The flaws and rough edges of Sophocles' characters were smoothed over, the characters drained of depth, and the interiority of the action that accompanies the inexorable movement toward matricide in Sophocles' play replaced with an adventure in the outer world.

Hugo von Hofmannstahl, Elektra *(1903)*

One hundred fifty-three years later, Hugo von Hofmannstahl's *Elektra* (1903) was performed in Berlin. Like Voltaire, Hofmannstahl credits Sophocles' *Electra* as his main source, and, like Voltaire's adaptation, his too was part of a wider project of adaptations of Classical Greek plays engaged in by the author and his contemporaries.

Hofmannstahl's interest in the classics was very different from Voltaire's. For Hofmannstahl, Greek tragedy was a repository of myth, which he saw as an avenue to the hidden, darker aspects of human nature. He was influenced by the rediscovery of the chthonic regions by the philosopher Nietzsche and by the new in-depth psychology. His library contained first editions of Breuer's and Freud's *Studies in Hysteria* (1895) and of Freud's *Interpretation of Dreams* (1900).

Hofmannstahl's *Elektra*, set in the courtyard of a palace in no identifiable time or place, focuses on the irrational and darker aspects of human nature. These were also present in Sophocles' *Electra*, but Hofmannstahl greatly accentuates them and removes from his play the rationality that had balanced them in Sophocles' treatment. He eliminates the Chorus, the voice of reason in Sophocles' play; pares back the role of the Paedagogus, the voice of practicality, to some five lines; and does not bring the pragmatic and opportunistic Orestes into the play until the last possible moment.

His adaptation features the three women in Sophocles' text, and draws them all as highly distraught and overwrought. Electra is an isolated, abused, and degraded figure, hated by all but one of the servants, who grasps her essential nobility. Beaten and nearly starved by her parents and forced to live with the dogs, she practically howls and barks as they do. Her greatest wish is to dance in victory around her father's grave after slaughtering his murderers. Chrysothemis has none of the prudence of the Sophoclean figure and is no less anguished or rebellious than her sister. She is a deeply frustrated woman who longs desperately for the normal life that is denied her. She wants to flee the claustrophobic palace where she is confined with Electra and passionately desires marriage and children. "I am a woman and desire a woman's fate" (p.17), she declares. Clytemnestra is a grotesque despot, covered with jewels and charms, and consumed by violent hatred of Electra and by the terror produced by her frightening dreams.

Hofmannstahl turns the *agôn* into an opportunity for mother and daughter to express the agony and rage that fill them. Clytemnestra demands that Electra reveal the "rites" that will put an end to her tormenting dreams and allow her to sleep again. Convinced that she will be relieved of her dreams "as soon as the right blood has flowed" (p.30), she is determined to "find out/ who must bleed so I can sleep again" (p.38), even if that means torturing Electra to extract the answer. Electra is no less malicious or bloody minded. Reveling in her mother's agony, she exacerbates it by telling Clytemnestra that she will be free of her dreams when "the right/ victim falls beneath the axe" (p.30) but refusing to say who that is. Then, enflamed by her mother's violent description of how she and Aegisthus will force the answer from her, Electra launches into her own blood-soaked description of the anticipated revenge:

> Who must bleed? Your own neck must bleed
> when the hunter has moved in for the kill!
> He will knife his game, but only on the run!   (p.38)

Hofmannstahl jettisons the moral concerns of Sophocles' play. His *Elektra* contains no discussion of the justice of Agamemnon's murder and offers no consensus (provided by the Chorus in Sophocles' play) regarding the justice of the children's vengeance. Sophocles treated the subject of memory as a moral issue: the child's duty to remember the murdered parent. Hofmannstahl treats it as a psychological issue. His Clytemnestra, who has repressed all recollection of her role in murdering Agamemnon, is tormented by her dreams and suffers from inner rot and chaos. His Electra, like her Sophoclean namesake, excoriates Chrysothemis for wanting to put the past behind her. She charges that it is bestial to shake off the past, implying that it is the ability to remember that makes one human. Yet it is her clinging to the memory of her father that causes Electra to sacrifice her happiness and humanity.

Like Sophocles' *Electra*, Hofmannstahl's is also rife with ambiguity. After Orestes kills Clytemnestra and Aegisthus, Electra goes into an ecstatic maenadic dance, which ends with her collapse and death. She has achieved her wish to dance on her father's grave. But the play does not indicate how we should view this ending. Is it the ultimate triumph or the ultimate defeat? Does it indicate that Electra has completed her life's work and has no more need to be around or that Chrysothemis' affirmation of life was the better path? The ambiguities in Sophocles' *Electra* reflected the gap between the ideal and its actualization in a world where every action has multiple meanings and consequences. The ambiguity on which Hofmannstahl's *Elektra* ends stems from Hofmannstahl's view that words are insufficient to convey meaning. For Hofmannstahl, meaning exists beyond words, in the fusion of gesture, ritual and myth that he sought in ancient Greek tragedy.

Hofmannstahl's *Elektra* was adapted by Richard Strauss (1864-1949) for operatic performance and performed in 1909.[4]

Jean Paul Sartre, The Flies (Les Mouches) *(1943)*

Jean Paul Sartre's *The Flies* combines elements of all three classical dramas. Harking back to Sophocles' version, it opens with Orestes' return, accompanied by his Tutor, to the city of his birth. As in Sophocles' version, the Tutor describes the life of the city to Orestes and the two ask for directions to Aegisthus' home. The depiction of Electra as a servant in her father's home and her pointed resemblance to her mother may also be traced to Sophocles' play. From Aeschylus' treatment are drawn the centrality of Orestes to the action of *The Flies* and the attack of the Furies following the murders. To

---

4   On Hofmannstahl's adaptation and Strauss' opera, see most recently Scott (2005) 25-43, 57-80, Bakogianni (2007), Goldhill (2002) and McDonald (2001) 115-131.

Euripides, Sartre owes his depiction of Electra as prodding the initially reluctant and uncertain Orestes to carry out the revenge.

The Flies was produced in 1943, when France was occupied by the Nazis and ruled by the puppet Vichy government. When writing the play, Sartre was actively involved both in the Resistance to the occupation and in formulating his existentialist philosophy. The year the play was produced he published his major philosophical work, *Being and Nothingness*, in which he insisted on the human being's freedom from all determinism. *The Flies* may be read as an expression of both his resistance politics and his existential philosophy.

Politically, *The Flies* is an allegory of German occupation and French collaboration. Aegisthus is a tyrant who has usurped the throne of the king he killed and oppresses his people. In clear allusions to the Nazis, he claims that he murdered Agamemnon to restore order and refers to Electra as "vermin"— the term the Nazis had applied to the Jews. The French people who collaborated with the Nazis are represented by the miserable, cowed, and guilt-ridden citizens of Argos, who allowed the murder to happen (and even welcomed it) and who accept Aegisthus as their ruler. The all-pervasive flies that afflict them in punishment for their complicity are compared to a pestilence, which may be understood as referring to the presence of German soldiers throughout occupied France. Orestes' killing of Argos' rulers may be read as the act of resistance required to free France from the German occupation.

The use of the myth enabled Sartre to avoid German censorship. To focus on his political message, he reduced Clytemnestra to a very minor character, omitted the references to her lust and sexuality that are prominent in the classical treatments, and foregrounded the motifs of Aegisthus' usurpation and tyranny that figure in both Aeschylus' and Sophocles' dramatizations.

Philosophically, the main theme of *The Flies* is human freedom. To deal with this theme, Sartre introduces the figure of Zeus, depicting him as a ridiculous and malicious god whose overriding aim is to subject humanity to his rule, and casts Aegisthus as Zeus's agent on earth. The power of religion (represented by Zeus) and the power of the state (represented by Aegisthus) support one another in hiding from human beings the fact that they are essentially free.

The plot traces Orestes' discovery and implementation of his freedom. The moment of discovery comes when Orestes rejects the guidance of Zeus, for which he himself had asked in his uncertainty and confusion. Although Zeus sent a sign showing that what he wanted was not the shedding of blood, but humility and acceptance of the state of affairs as it was, Orestes determines to set out on his own path. At that moment, Orestes changes from a gentle youth to a determined individual who acts on his convictions. All the other characters are shown failing to realize their freedom. Aegisthus is the least free, because he must maintain an image of power so as to conceal from his subjects the knowledge of their freedom. In the end, he loses himself and is so sick of life that he offers no resistance to Orestes' axe. The Tutor, who has raised Orestes as a skeptic free of the fear and tyranny of religion, represents the intellectual whose freedom is limited because it is not accompanied by commitment and action. Electra turns her back on her freedom. She was driven to urge the murders and to serve as an accomplice by her hatred and desire for revenge. Once the revenge is accomplished, she feels empty and falls prey to the "Furies of remorse" and to the flies that now become their symbol. To alleviate her remorse, she accepts Zeus's offer of protection if she agrees to repent. This she does, repudiating Orestes, who urges her to reject the offer.

Orestes emerges as the only character who lives his freedom. He is free because he acts on convictions independently arrived at. Convinced that the right thing for him to do is to free the people of Argos, he is certain of the moral rightness of his "crime" and feels no remorse. His freedom has its price. He is abhorrent to Zeus (the religious establishment), rejected by the townspeople whom he has liberated from a tyrant, and repudiated by his sister. The hope of finding a place among the people of his city that brought him to Argos is dashed, and he leaves the city to continue on his lonely way. However, he is no longer the aimless wanderer he had been before he came to Argos, but a man who will follow his own path, true to himself.

John Barton, The Greeks *(1980)*

John Barton's adaptation of Sophocles' *Electra* is the sixth play in his ten-play cycle entitled *The Greeks*. As Barton describes it (p.vii), *The Greeks* is a single work performed over three evenings that tells the story of the fall of the house of Atreus, which is also the story of the fall of a civilization. Of the ten plays, *Electra* is one of only three that is not derived from Euripides (though it borrows many elements of Euripides' treatment). Like the other plays in the cycle, it was constructed to fit into the ongoing narrative and is best appreciated in connection with the other adaptations. For reasons of focus and space, the links with the other plays will not be pursued here.

Much like Voltaire, Barton, a British playwright, director, and advisor to the Royal Shakespeare Company, wanted to make Greek tragedy accessible to contemporary audiences. In his view, current translations and performances were too "heavy, earnest, ritualistic, portentous, and not *human*" (p.vii). In *The Greeks*, he and Kenneth Cavander, the translator with whom he collaborated, set out to correct these flaws.

The play, scheduled to take forty-five minutes on stage, is highly condensed so as to fit into a theater evening with two other plays. The terse, pithy style and the removal of the repetitions that characterize Sophocles' tragedies also reflect the "simple, lucid, and terse translation and…light, non-indulgent, non-tragic production style" to which Barton and Cavander aspired (p. vii). The adaptation focuses on the plot of the play so as to familiarize the modern theater-goer, uneducated in the classics, with the myth, while tempering the emotional intensity of Electra's rancor, the grotesque egotism and abusiveness of Clytemnestra, the elation in the recognition scene, and the horror of the matricide. The result is a down-to-earth rendition, which can be described either as *unburdened* by the great philosophic and emotional weight that characterizes Sophocles' play or as *lacking* in these dimensions and in the depth they provide.

Like Voltaire, Barton acknowledged the derivation of his play from Sophocles' *Electra*, while making extensive changes. Voltaire's motive was to shape his characters in accord with contemporary notions of the hero, Barton's to make his characters "human"—which meant for Barton that they were full of contradictions and inconsistencies, and that none was all good or all bad.

Thus, his Clytemnestra is a wife who killed her husband in a fit of jealousy when he brought home another woman. She has little good to say about Agamemnon, but there are hints that she once loved him in her statement to Electra: "Nothing in this world/ Hurts a woman / More than to love and to be hurt" (p.162). Nor is she nearly as bad a mother as her Sophoclean namesake. She is relieved to be free of Orestes' threat on her life, but she does not pray to Apollo that harm come to him and Electra, only that she live with "children who do not hate me" (p.166). The implication is that she would welcome Orestes' and Electra's affection.

His Orestes (whose characterization follows Euripides') is weak, indecisive, and prodded to the matricide by Electra. But he is also fully a murderer, who self-righteously rejects Clytemnestra's pleas for pity with the angry retort that she had never pitied him. Barton's Electra shares the bloody-minded ferocity of Sophocles' character, as she echoes the chilling call of her Sophoclean namesake to Orestes to "strike [Clytemnestra] again" (p.178). Yet she is a much more ambivalent character than the single-minded Electra of Sophocles' play. Toward the end of the adaptation, Barton's Electra looks at her mother's corpse and tells her: "you were the one I loved/ And you were the one I hated" (p.82). Sophocles' Electra never expressed any love for her mother.

Along with these changes in characterization, Barton also revised the ending of Sophocles' *Electra*. Sophocles' play ends with Orestes leading Aegisthus into the palace to be killed. The avengers are uncontrite and firm in their belief in the rightness of their deed, and the Chorus declare that the vengeance has brought freedom to Agamemnon's descendants. Leaving Sophocles and borrowing heavily from Euripides, Barton extends the ending to include the murder of Aegisthus and the aftermath of the killings.

In this aftermath, he shows the avengers uncertain and remorseful and the Chorus confused. Right after the murders, Barton's avengers realize that they have committed a terrible crime. Looking at Clytemnestra's and Aegisthus' corpses, they suddenly feel isolated and afraid. Each asks "where can I go now?" (p.181). Orestes continues, "Who will bear to look at me,/ The man who killed his mother?" Electra says: "No one will dance with me,/ No one will marry me,/ No one will take me into his bed." Orestes tries to convince himself of the rightness of his deed by citing Apollo's command: "One thing justifies me, Apollo made me do it" (p.182). But Electra is skeptical. "Can we trust what he tells us?" she asks and goes on to contemplate the possibility that "Apollo was wrong" (p.182). In their last statements, Orestes sees the Furies pursuing him, and Electra desperately prays to Apollo to "Let the curse on our house/ Have some end" (p.183) — a prayer which implies that it well may not.

The Chorus initially echo the closing song in Sophocles' play, assuring the avengers that: "You have both done justly./ You have freed the throne" (p.181), and respond to the avengers' doubts with the positivistic counsel: "… Be strong of heart./ Be happy, It is over./ Justice has prevailed" (p.182). But in their exit song, they raise the most basic questions, not only about whether the revenge was right or wrong and whether it did or did not attain its end, but about the nature of Good and Evil:

What shall we say of this?
Are we free from evil?
Or caught in more evil?
What is Good and Evil?
I do not know.   (p.183)

Barton's changes in characterization are in the spirit of Sophocles, who also endowed most of his protagonists with an assortment of qualities that do not always fit well together. Sophocles' Orestes, Electra, and Chrysothemis all show contradictions in thinking and/or behavior, as well as a mixture of virtues and defects. Even Sophocles' Clytemnestra has moments in which she is not entirely evil, as her maternal feelings briefly emerge before they are overcome by her terror for her life. We also find in Sophocles' play the lack of resolution that marks Barton's ending. It is not only that none of the debates in Sophocles' play can be clearly resolved in favor of one side over the other; it is also that Sophocles' play ends on a disturbing note, such that it is difficult to envision the avengers living happily ever after, even if justice has been done and they are free of the usurpers' tyranny.

But nothing in Sophocles matches the question of Barton's Chorus: "What is Good and Evil?" In Sophocles' play we find moral complexity: justice is achieved when the evil of Agamemnon's murder is punished, albeit by the evils of murder and matricide. The horrors of the vengeance bring home the abyss between the ideal and its attainment. But justice, nonetheless, remains an ideal. In Barton's play we find moral confusion. Barton's changes in characterization, especially Clytemnestra's, give his audience reason to doubt the justice of the vengeance, while the Chorus' question effectively undermines the notion that we can know what is and is not just and even that Justice or any other ideal actually exists.

Beyond rendering the narrative of "the Electra myth" accessible to modern audiences, the point of Barton's adaptation is to bring out this uncertainty and moral confusion. In Barton's view, it is precisely such moral confusion and uncertainty that mark civilizations in their decline and that link Sophocles' age to our own (p.ix). To make this point, Barton departs from his usual practice of condensing events as much as possible and substantially lengthens Sophocles' ending.

The Electra Complex and the Repudiation of Electra

The concept of Electra that seems to derive from Sophocles' depiction goes by the name of "the Electra Complex." This concept was introduced into twentieth-century thinking by the famous psychoanalyst Carl Jung in 1912 in his book *Freud and Psychoanalysis*:

> …a daughter develops a specific liking for her father, with a correspondingly jealous attitude towards the mother. As everyone knows, Electra took vengeance on her mother Clytemnestra for murdering her husband Agamemnon and thus robbing her – Electra – of her beloved father. (p.154)

Jung does not acknowledge a debt to any of the ancient playwrights, but takes his account of Electra as common knowledge. It is an inaccurate account in that in none of the known classical versions of the myth did Electra herself take vengeance on her mother. This was always Orestes' task, and Electra was his accomplice.

Nonetheless, it may be suggested that Jung's dual image of Electra as a woman who loves her father and hates her mother and as a violent woman who kills her mother can be traced back to Sophocles' treatment. It is Euripides' Clytemnestra who states that some children love their fathers more, others their mothers (*Electra* 1101-104). But it is Sophocles' play that is dominated by Electra, his play in which her deep grief for her murdered father and hatred for her mother are given the greatest emphasis, and his play in which her running commentary on the murders nearly makes her an accomplice.

Although Freud regarded Jung's formulations as redundant and Jung himself ignored the Electra complex in his later writings, it has become a key element of psycho-analytic theory and a widely known concept that has fired the popular imagination through much of the twentieth century and beyond. Since it appears in many works of literature that are not specifically based on Sophocles' play — or on Aeschylus' or Euripides' either — the debt to Sophocles goes unacknowledged. The writer may even be unaware of it.

Eugene O'Neill, Mourning Becomes Electra

The Electra complex is central to Eugene O'Neill's trilogy, *Mourning Becomes Electra*, first produced in 1931. O'Neill's trilogy, set in New England after the Civil War, is a drama about the cross-currents of sexuality in the family, with its attendant jealousy, violence, and guilt. Structurally, it follows Aeschylus' *Oresteia*, with the key event in each play corresponding to the key event in the parallel play by Aeschylus.

Yet, whereas Electra is a secondary character in Aeschylus' trilogy, appearing only in the *Libation Bearers*, and there only briefly, O'Neill's Electra character, Lavinia, holds a central place in all three of his plays. In the first, *The Homecoming*, she is already shown to hate her sexually attractive mother and be incestuously attached to her father even before his murder at the end of the play. In the second, *The Hunted* (which harks back to Euripides' portrayal), she goads her weak and indecisive brother to kill her mother's lover for his role in the murder, which, in turn, leads to her mother's suicide. In the third, *The Haunted*, she briefly flourishes after her father's murderers have been killed, but is soon ravaged by the same guilt that wracks her brother Orin and causes him to take his life.

O'Neill's Lavinia is a repressed, embittered, and manipulative woman who brings a great deal of grief to her family and others around her. In treating the conduct of his Electra character as a psychological disturbance rather than as a quest for justice, O'Neill essentially removes sympathy for her and, in tandem, draws her mother, his Clytemnestra character, Christine Mammon, more sympathetically. Much like the traditional Clytemnestra, his Christine is a selfish and manipulative woman, an adulterous and murderous wife, and a mother who is hostile and callous toward her daughter, though, here, she loves her Oedipal son. But O'Neill anchors the causes for her conduct in the hardness of her husband, Ezra Mammon (i.e. Agamemnon), and the hostility of her daughter who vies with her for his love.

The Repudiation

Subsequent writers go further in repudiating Electra. Marilyn Hacker, in a poem titled "For Elektra," repudiates the masculine ways of the Electra figure. The poem begins with the natural death of the narrator's (presumably Hacker's) father and with her mother, who "did not kill or save him," standing above him "like a small/ vulture in curlers." She describes Electra as a dyke, a "Lustful shorthaired virgin/ bitch" who, assuming her brother's voice, tells her "Your mother is my mother. Dare." She, however, declares: "I would rather make love and poems than kill/ my mother."

In H.D.'s (Hilda Doolittle) poem "Electra-Orestes," Electra is a woman who has turned evil and whose heart "thrives on hate." Electra tries to fathom how the hate develops in "the heart of the child," who starts out full of love, and Orestes asks her much the same question. The poem never provides a clear answer, though it hints that the murderous hatred that grew up in her was somehow a product of love, longing, and jealousy. "To love, one must slay," Electra declares in the poem's opening line. The poem ends with a Choral statement — *"woe, woe for those who spent/ life-blood / in hate"* — that conveys both sympathy and censure for Electra, as the woman who was responsible for her mother's death and who wasted her own life in her hatred for her.

John Barton treats Electra again in his play *Tantalus*, published in 2000 and premiered in Denver, Colorado in October, 2000. Like *The Greeks* (1981), it is a massive work that tells the story of Agamemnon's house before, during, and after the Trojan War, in ten plays. The events that Barton chose to recount are recorded in the summaries of the long lost *Epic Cycle*, but his take on them is entirely his own, driven by his attempt to figure out "what is the truth of it." His answer, revealed in his extensive revisions of the stories, is that the events were driven by a combination of stupidity, fecklessness, and the baser passions—lust, greed, jealousy, anger, and so on. Characterization, motives and events are all changed out of recognition in accordance with this view. Electra is drawn as an angry young woman overly fond of her father and at loggerheads with her mother well before the Greek fleet sets out for Troy. After her father is murdered, she spreads the rumor that her mother was responsible for his death and, as in Sophocles' play, hounds the exiled Orestes with letters demanding that he return to avenge their father's murder.

Over the centuries, Sophocles' *Electra* has been a popular play, both in translation and adaptation. The idealism and passion of Sophocles' heroine and the deeply rooted psychological dynamics she portrays make her a rich and expressive character to act, a riveting character on stage, and a versatile figure who lends herself to both political and psychological treatment. The above discussion may give some idea of the many ways in which playwrights have seen Sophocles' heroine and the play as a whole.

BIBLIOGRAPHY

Alexiou, M. *The Ritual Lament in Greek Tradition,* 2nd ed, revised by Dimitrios Yatromanolakis and Panagiotis Roilos (Lanham, MD: Rowman & Littlefield, c2002)

Bailey, C., E.A. Barber, C.M. Bowra, J.D. Denniston, and D.L. Page, eds. *Greek Poetry and Life: Essays Presented to Gilbert Murray on his Seventieth Birthday* (Oxford: Oxford University Press, 1936)

Bakogianni, A. "An Eighteenth-Century Jealous Woman and a Twentieth-Century Hysterical Diva: The Case of Mozart's *Idomeneo* (1781) and Strauss's *Elektra* (1909)," *New Voices in Classical Reception Studies* Issue 2 (2007) 1-33

Barrett, J. *Staged Narrative: Poetics and the Messenger in Greek Tragedy* (Berkeley: University of California Press, 2002)

Barton, J. and K. Cavander. *The Greeks: Ten Plays Given as a Trilogy* (London: Heinemann, 1981)

-------------- *Tantalus: An Ancient Myth for a New Millennium* (London: Oberon Books, 2000)

Batchelder, A.G. *The Seal of Orestes: Self-reference and Authority in Sophocles' Electra* (Lanham, MD: Rowman & Littlefield, c1995)

Burnett, A.P. *Revenge in Attic and Later Tragedy* (Berkeley: University of California Press, 1998)

Buxton, R.G.A. *Persuasion in Greek Tragedy* (Cambridge, New York: Cambridge University Press, 1982)

-------------- *Sophocles.* Greece and Rome New Surveys in the Classics, No. 16 (Oxford: Clarendon Press, 1984)

Cairns, D.L. *Aidôs: the Psychology and Ethics of Honour and Shame in Ancient Greek Literature* (Oxford: Clarendon Press; New York: Oxford University Press, 1993).

Carson, A. "Screaming in Translation: The *Elektra* of Sophokles," in *Sophocles' "Electra" in Performance*, ed. F.D. Dunn (Stuttgart: M & P, 1996), 5-11

Csapo, E. and W.J. Slater. *The Context of Ancient Drama* (Ann Arbor: University of Michigan Press, 1995)

Damen, M. "Actor and Character in Greek Tragedy," *Theatre Journal* 41 (1989) 316-340.

Davidson, J., F. Muecke, P. Wilson (eds.). *Greek Drama III: Essays in Honour of Kevin Lee* (London: Institute of Classical Studies, 2006).

Davies, M. (ed.) *Epicorum Graecorum Fragmenta* (Göttingen: Vandenhoek & Ruprecht, c. 1988)

Dominik, W.J. "Africa," in *A Companion to Classical Tradition*, ed. C.W. Kallendorf (Oxford: Blackwell, 2007) 117-131

Dunn, F.M. (ed.) *Sophocles' "Electra" in Performance* (Stuttgart: M & P, 1996)

Easterling, P. and E. Hall (eds.) *Greek and Roman Actors: Aspects of an Ancient Profession* (Cambridge: Cambridge University Press, 2002)

Flashar, H. *Inszenierung der Antike: das griechishe Drama auf der Bühne der Neuzeit 1585-1990* (Munich: C.H. Beck, 1991).

Garland, R. *The Greek Way of Death*, 2nd edition (Ithaca, NY: Cornell University Press, 2001)

Gellie, G.H. *Sophocles: A Reading* (Carlton, Victoria: Melbourne University Press, 1972)

Goldhill, S. *Who Needs Greek: Contests in the Cultural History of Hellenism* (Cambridge: Cambridge University Press, 2002) 108-177

Goward, B. *Telling Tragedy: Narrative Technique in Aeschylus, Sophocles & Euripides* (Duckworth, 2004)

Grene, D. *Sophocles*. Translated and with Introduction. 2nd ed. (Chicago: University of Chicago Press, 1991)

Griffin, J. "Sophocles and the Democratic City," in J. Griffin. (ed.) *Sophocles Revisited: Essays Presented to Sir Hugh Lloyd-Jones* (Oxford: Oxford University Press, 1999) 73-94

---------- (ed.) *Sophocles Revisited: Essays Presented to Sir Hugh Lloyd-Jones* (Oxford: Oxford University Press, 1999)

Hacker, M. *Selected Poems, 1965-1990* (New York: Norton, 1994)

Hall, E. "The Singing Actors of Antiquity," in P. Easterling and E. Hall (eds.) *Greek and Roman Actors* (Cambridge: Cambridge University Press, 2002) 3-38

-------------- and F. Macintosh. *Greek Tragedy and the British Theatre 1660-1914* (Oxford: Oxford University Press, 2005)

Hartigan, K.V. *Greek Tragedy on the American Stage: Ancient Drama in the Commercial Theater, 1882-1994* (Westport, Connecticut; London: Greenwood Press, 1995)

-------------- "Resolution without Victory / Victory without Resolution: The Identification Scene in Sophocles' *Electra*," in F.D. Dunn (ed.) *Sophocles' "Electra" in Performance*, (Stuttgart: M & P, 1996) 82-92

H.D. (Hilda Doolittle) *Collected Poems, 1912-1944.* Ed. Louis L. Martz. (New York: New Directions, 1983)

Hofmannstahl, Hugo von. *Elektra*, Trans by A. Schwarz, in *Selected Plays and Libretti* by H. von Hofmannstahl. Edited and introduced by Michael Hamburger (New York: Pantheon Books, c1963) 3-77

Hogan, J.C. *A Commentary on the Plays of Sophocles* (Carbondale and Edwardsville: Southern Illinois University Press, 1991)

Jebb, R.C. *Sophocles: Plays. Electra* (Bristol Classical Press, 2004 [1894])

Jory, D.H. *Oreste* in *The Complete Works of Voltaire* (Oxford: The Voltaire Foundation Taylor Institution, 1992), vol. 31A, 320-335.

Juffras, D.M. "Sophocles' *Electra* 973-85 and Tyrannicide," *TAPhA* 121(1991) 99-108

Jung, C.G. *Freud and Psychoanalysis.* Trans by R.F.C. Hull (New York: Pantheon Books, 1961)

Kallendorf, C.W. (ed.) *A Companion to Classical Tradition* (Oxford: Blackwell, 2007)

Kamerbeek, J.C. *The Plays of Sophocles, Part V: The Electra* (Leiden: Brill, 1974)

Kells, J.H. *Sophocles: Electra* (Cambridge: Cambridge University Press, 1973)

Kirkwood, G.M. *A Study of Sophoclean Drama, with a new Preface and Enlarged Bibliographical Note* (Ithaca and London: Cornell University Press, 1994)

Kitto, H.D.F. *Poiesis: Structure and Thought* (Berkley: University of California Press, 1966)

Kurtz, D.C. and J. Boardman. *Greek Burial Customs* (Ithaca, NY, 1971)

Ley, G. *A Short Introduction to the Ancient Greek Theater* (Chicago and London: The University of Chicago Press, 2006 revised edition)

Lloyd, M. *Sophocles: Electra* (London: Duckworth, 2005)

MacLeod, L. *Dolos and Dike in Sophokles'* Elektra. (Leiden, Boston, Köln: Brill, 2001)

March, J. "The Chorus in Sophocles' *Electra*," in *Sophocles' "Electra" in Performance*, ed. F.D. Dunn (Stuttgart: M & P, 1996) 65-81

-------------- *Sophocles: Electra.* (Warminster: Aris & Pillips, 2001)

Marshall, C.W. "How to Write a Messenger Speech (Sophocles, *Electra* 680-763)." *Greek Drama III: Essays in Honour of Kevin Lee*, eds. J. Davidson, F. Muecke, P. Wilson (London: Institute of Classical Studies, 2006) 203-21.

McDonald, M. *Sing Sorrow: Classics, History, and Heroines in Opera* (Westport, CT; London: Greenwood Press, 2001)

Merkelbach, R. and M.L. West (eds.). *Fragmenta Hesiodea* (Oxford: Oxford University Press, 1967)

Minadeo, R. "Plot, Theme, and Meaning in Sophocles' *Electra*," *Class. et Med.* 28(1967) 114-142

O'Neill, E. *Mourning Becomes Electra* in *Nine Plays by Eugene O'Neill* (New York: Liveright, Inc., 1931) 687-867

Owen, A.S. "The Date of the *Electra* of Sophocles," in *Greek Poetry and Life*. *Essays Presented to Gilbert Murray on his Seventieth Birthday, January 2, 1936* (Oxford: The Clarendon Press, 1936) 145-157

Pavlovskis, Z. "The Voice of the Actor in Greek Tragedy," *CW* 71 (1977) 113-123

Pickard-Cambridge, A. *The Dramatic Festivals of Athens*, 2nd ed. Revised by J. Gould and D.M. Lewis (Oxford: Clarendon Press, 1988)

Prag, A.J.N.W. *The Oresteia: Iconographic and Narrative Tradition* (Chicago, Ill: Bolchazy-Carducci, c1985)

Ringer, M. "Reflections on an Empty Urn," in F.D. Dunn (ed.) *Sophocles' "Electra" in Performance* (Stuttgart: M & P, 1996) 93-100

-------------- *Electra and the Empty Urn: Metatheater and Role Playing in Sophocles* (Chapel Hill and London: The University of North Carolina, 1998)

Roisman, H.M. "Hesiod's *Ate*," *Hermes* 111(1983) 491-496

------------- "*Ate* and its Meaning in the Elegies of Solon," *Grazer Beiträge* 11(1984) 21-27

-------------- "Hesiod's *Ate* Again," *SCI* VIII-IX(1985) 11-15

-------------- "Meter and Meaning," *NECJ* 27.4 (2000) 182-199

Russo, J., Fernandez-Galiano, M., Heubeck, A. *A Commentary on Homer's Odyssey*. Vol. III, Books xvii-xxiv. (Oxford: Clarendon Press, 1992)

Sartre, J-P. *The Flies* (Les Mouches). Trans. from French by S. Gilbert, in *No Exit and Three Other Plays*. (New York: Vintage Books, 1960) 51-127

Schein, L.S. "*Electra*: A Sophoclean Problem Play," *Antike und Abendland* 28(1982) 69-80

Scott, J. *Electra after Freud* (Ithaca and London: Cornell University Press, 2005)

Segal, C. "The *Electra* of Sophocles, " *TAPhA* 97(1966) 473-545

-------------- "Visual Symbolism and Visual Effects in Sophocles," *CW* 74(1980/1981) 125-142. Reprinted in Segal 1986.

-------------- *Interpreting Greek Tragedy: Myth, Poetry, Text* (Ithaca and London: Cornell University Press, 1986)

Sheppard, J.T. "Electra: a Defense of Sophocles," *CR* 41(1927) 2-9

-------------- "Electra again," *CR* 41 (1927) 163-165

Sommerstein, A.H. "Alternative Scenarios in Sophocles' *Electra*," *Prometheus* 23(1997) 193-214

-------------- *Greek Drama and Dramatists* (London, New York: Routledge, 2002)

Sourvinou-Inwood, C. *"Reading" Greek Death* (Oxford: Clarendon Press, 1995)

Sutton, D.F. *The Greek Satyr Play* (Meisenheim am Glan: Anton Hain, 1980)

Taplin, O. *Greek Tragedy in Action* (Berkeley and Los Angeles: University of California Press, 1978)

van Erp Taalman Kip, A.M. "Truth in Tragedy: When Are We Entitled to Doubt Character's Words?" *AJP* 117(1996) 517-536

Voltaire. *The Works of Voltaire: a Contemporary Version.* A critique & biography by the Rt. Hon. John Morley ; notes by Tobias Smollett ; rev. and modernized, new translations by William F. Fleming and an introduction by Oliver H.G. Leigh, vol. xvii (Paris: E.R. DuMont, 1901)

Walton, J.M. "Sophocles' *Electra*: Actors in Space," in *Sophocles' "Electra" in Performance*, ed. F.D. Dunn (Stuttgart: M & P, 1996) 41-48

Wiles, D. *Tragedy in Athens: Performance Space and Theatrical Meaning* (Cambridge: Cambridge University Press, 1997)

Wilson, P. *The Athenian Institution of the* Khoregia: *The Chorus, the City and the Stage* (Cambridge: Cambridge University Press, 2000)

Winnington-Ingram, R.P. *Sophocles: An Interpretation* (Cambridge: Cambridge University Press, 1980)

Woodard, T. "The Electra of Sophocles," in T. Woodard (ed.) *Sophocles: A Collection of Essays* (Englewood Cliffs, NJ: Prentice Hall, 1966) 125-145

-------------- (ed.) *Sophocles: A Collection of Critical Essays* (Englewood Cliffs, NJ: Prentice Hall, 1966)

-------------- "*Electra* by Sophocles: the Dialectical Design," *HSCP* 68 (1965) 163-205 and 70(1965) 195-233

INDEX

The numbers in bold reflect line or passage numbers. Plain numbers refer to page numbers, 'n' preceding a number, e.g., n20 means note/s on p. 20.